How to be a decent
DPO

MARTIN HOSKINS

HOW TO BE A DECENT DPO

CONTENTS

ACKNOWLEDGMENTS

I could not have progressed as I have in my long data protection career without being motivated and inspired by a good number of privacy pros. While I could never bring myself to wholeheartedly agree with all their views, these people have helped me realise, from a data protection perspective, what is important and what is not. What values are necessary to uphold and what character traits should be avoided. How to present your arguments in a compelling manner and how not.

I will mention by name some key people who have especially helped me develop as a privacy pro. Without their influence, these letters would have taken a very different tone. They are: Robert Armstrong, Emma Ascroft, Roma Avrili, Jon Baines, Andy Beet, Paul Bernal, Heather Bignell-Blye, Simon Blanchard, Richard Boase, Robert Bond, Iain Bourne, Neil Brown, Nick Brown, Emma Butler, Robin Butler, Colin Caldwell, Anthony Campion, Joanna Cavan, Kasey Chappelle, Virginia Chinda-Coutts, Mabel Choo, Carmel Codd, Michael Collon, Jenny Coombs, Sue Cullen, Stephen Deadman, Phil Donn, Robin Dormer, Stephen Douglas, Stewart Dresner, David Erdos, Dave Evans, Paul Fennelly, Yvonne Fern, Elizabeth France, Shelagh Gaskill, Sue Gold, Hazel Grant, Christopher Graham, Nick Graham, Hazel Grant, James Leaton Gray, Michael Hallowes, Charlotte Harper, Liza Hee, Henry Hirsch, Alice Holt, Robin Hopkins, Gus Hosein, Trevor Hughes, Julian Huppert, Dave Johnston, Elaine Johnson-Smith, Alan Jones, Jim Killock, Eric King, Andrew Knight, Christopher Knight, John Kropf, Xavier Leclerc, Reynold Leming, David Maclean, Julia Makara, William Malcolm, Hamish MacLeod, Stephen McCartney, Simon McDougal, TJ McIntyre, Nicola McKilligan-Regan, Christopher Millard, Charles Miller, Mita Mitra, Vanessa Mortiaux, Paul Murphy, Daragh & Ralph

Obrien, Rachel O'Connell, Jess Ong, Emily Overton, Guy Perring, Ellis Perry, Nick Pickles, Timothy Pitt-Payne, Jules Polonetsky, Julia Porter, Chris & William Pounder, Anya Proops, Dan Raywood, David Reynolds, Stewart Room, Peter Roth, Ian Roy, Duncan Sagar, Linda Sheppard, Ollie Simpson, Laurie Slade, David Smith, three people named Graham Smith, Peter Sommer, Elizabeth Stafford, Fiona Stapleton, Toby Stevens, Valerie Taylor, Richard Thomas, Tim Turner, Nick Tyler, Claus Ulmer, Ian Waldman, Pat Walshe, Christopher Williams, Paula Williamson, Christopher Wolf, Jack Wraith, Jacquie Yang & Zhi Hao Yong.

I also thank colleagues in many of the organisations I've known or have worked with during my career for their helping me realise that data protection risks vary so very greatly, and that the same risk can have very different consequences, depending on the organisation. A one size approach definitely does not fit all. Data protection advice is best delivered in ways that are tailored to the specific needs of the organisation. They include: Amberhawk Training, Association of British Insurers, Association of Chief Police Officers, Barclays Bank, Bird & Bird, Bristol Water, British Bankers Association, British Computer Society, Cabinet Office, Commission for Energy Regulation (Ireland), Data Protection Forum, Data Protection Forum, Data Protection Network, Department of Energy, Communications & Natural Resources (Ireland), Digital Rights Ireland, DP Recruitment Ltd, EE (formerly One-2-One, T-Mobile & Everything Everywhere), Experian, Finance UK, Financial Ombudsman Service, Friends Life, Future of Privacy Forum, Gemserv, Grant Thornton, Hill Dickinson, Home Office, Hutchison 3G UK, Hysteria Trust, Information Commissioner's Office, INHOPE, International Association of Privacy Professionals, Jaguar Land Rover, Kobalt, Lan3, Lloyds Bank, Marketforce, Meggitt, Migrant Help, Ministry of Justice, Monzo, MS Society, National Association of Data Protection Officers, Oxford Brooks University, Power to Change, Privacy Laws & Business, RSPCA, Save the Children, Security Awareness Special Interest

Group, Sickly, Simply Business, Sprint Communications, Standard Chartered Bank, Stirling Group, Terrence Higgins Trust, Tesco, Toyota Financial Services, UK intelligence agencies, UK Parliament & Wonde.

Finally, I am most grateful to all those whose comments and observations are reflected in this book. Decent Data Protection Officers recycle decent approaches to privacy. While the *italic text* and the endnotes endeavour to acknowledge the key contributions, I apologise to those whose insights have not been appropriately recognised. I could not have written these letters without them. I take full responsibility for all errors and trust that you won't find me too unreliable a narrator.

HOW TO BE A DECENT DPO

INTRODUCTION

These fourteen letters are designed to support you, a new entrant to the data protection field. It's a busy field, populated by noisy opinion formers who broadcast their views on an extremely wide range of privacy matters. Don't be put off by all the noise, though. Focus on what really matters – mastering the basic building blocks of the privacy ecosphere. Don't be put off by the ever-changing laws, drafted by policy makers that struggle to keep up with the innovative ways that organisations process personal data. As parliaments around the world pass increasingly complicated data protection laws, organisations are expected to both understand and be capable of evidencing how they meet the obligations that relate to them. This task is well beyond the capability of employees who have only a limited knowledge of data protection law and good practice. Increasingly, organisations need to engage with experienced privacy professionals. These professionals may be external consultants but, more likely, will be internal employees. They may work alone, or they may work in (mostly) small teams liaising with others who, perhaps in addition to reporting to other managers when performing some of their tasks, will also work under the direction of the Data Protection Officer ("DPO").

Don't' be put off by the huge the skills gap in the data protection world. It's no secret that the demand for data protection skills massively outweighs the supply, not just at entry-level but also for the more senior roles. Don't be put off when the resource problem gets worse. It's a problem that leads to an increasing number of people being appointed to positions with key data protection responsibilities even though they feel, to varying degrees, underprepared for the issues that they are expected to deal with.

It's not always the DPO's fault that they are unprepared for their appointment. It's not easy to find practical advice on what a DPO should do and how they should go about their work. There are many legal books, articles and blogs that explain in considerable detail what national data protection laws say, but few comment in any detail on what it is that data protection supervisory authorities are focused on, and even fewer explain how a busy DPO should prioritise their workload.

What are the essential tasks that a decent DPO must focus on immediately after their appointment, and what tasks can be left for another day? Also, given the amount of work that is often required to be done, and the relatively meagre resources that may be available to the DPO, what tasks could be left undone – and left to the DPO's eventual successor?

I've seen senior executives, particularly in the regulated industries, grandly announce that they have no appetite for risk, that their organisation must meet all of its legal obligations, and then fail to approve the expenditure that is necessary to deliver what is required. In my experience, very few of these executives appreciate what effort is required to ensure that their organisation meets all its data protection obligations. Many DPOs have struggled to explain to their senior management teams where their organisation is lacking, and what investment is necessary to address the deficiencies. Getting data protection right is a huge task for many organisations – particularly for those that have experienced decades of underinvestment in the privacy compliance field. Until very recently, data protection simply hasn't been sufficiently important an issue to warrant too much senior management time being spent on it. But, in light of recent regulatory mega-fines for non-compliance, senior management teams have been taking a much closer interest. Unfortunately, data protection compliance isn't as easy to achieve as most senior management teams might wish it to be. Nor is it something that can be achieved at little cost. Compliance is expensive. It also takes time and a lot of sustained commitment.

Drawing on over 30 years of operational data protection experience, here are my views on how a privacy professional should approach their work; what a busy DPO should do to comply with the really important areas of data protection law and practice; and what areas can be given less attention as deficiencies in these areas are far less likely to result in any individuals being harmed. I'm far more concerned about reducing the likelihood of individuals being harmed than I am in ensuring that every administrative requirement is met and evidenced with mountains of documentation.

These letters aren't always the product of my deep original thought. Sometimes, you may think that they are more of an attempt to assemble and interpret existing guidance, much of which has already been published and is readily available on the Internet. I'm here to help you gain a better understanding of what decent data protection behaviours look like. When I'm directly referring to the work of other people, I tend to use *italic text*. Otherwise, these thoughts are my own.

I don't expect that all my fellow data protection professionals will agree with my advice. There do exist high priests (and divas) of data protection, a select few of whom believe that every utterance by anyone attached to a data protection supervisory authority should be immediately actioned without question, and that compliance with every aspect of every data protection law is an absolute necessity. Others will disagree with me because we have a profound difference of view about when it is right that individuals should be left alone.

A noisy privacy industry exists, inhabited by consultants and organisations selling lots of services, tools and privacy tech. For these people, privacy is a business opportunity. The complexity of local data protection laws presents them and the organisations they work for with a great opportunity to sell stuff. Said stuff will be sold as 'privacy solutions.' Whether your organisation will find many of these solutions effective, desirable, or even necessary is questionable. They will be marketed as tools to make you, the DPO's, life easier and will be sold with assurances that the successful deployment of said tools will reduce the risk of huge fines being imposed by data protection supervisory authorities if your organisation does not comply with its legal obligations. The extremely detailed and prescriptive European data protection laws, flowing from the European Union's General Data Protection Regulation ("GDPR") for example, have provided the privacy industry with a great opportunity to spread concern amongst responsible organisations at the potential financial costs of getting data protection wrong. But not everyone is persuaded. Considering the patchy regulatory enforcement, albeit with the occasional eye-popping fine, increasing numbers of DPOs are questioning whether the financial risks their organisations face really are as great as is claimed by the privacy industry.

Decent DPOs should follow my approach and adopt a pragmatic approach to compliance with data protection laws. We pragmatists deal with things sensibly and realistically, in ways that are based on practical rather than theoretical considerations. This is an approach that is based on the premise that citizens and organisations don't always change their behaviours just because a new law has been passed. Politicians have a habit of grandstanding, of passing laws that impose standards that are, in practice, hard to meet. Politicians also have a habit of not concerning themselves too much about how strictly the laws they pass should be enforced. In the UK, at least, their reputations are not great. They know that they are unlikely to be in politics (or in power) for long enough for people and organisations to change their behaviours meet the requirements of the new laws.

Laws can be passed to reflect the political pressures of the day. 'Something' needs to be done. But those passing the laws, and those advising those who pass the laws, often don't always have the time to properly consult those that have specialist knowledge about how individuals will be affected by the laws. Sometimes, even the experts, who ought to know, may not fully appreciate the real implications of what has been proposed until the law has been enacted and it is too late to change its text.

So, these letters focus on what you should do, rather than what you should know. Data protection law, thanks to the decisions that are being made in courts and administrative tribunals, is changing at a frightening speed, and there is a real risk that much of the law that I will refer to will change. Therefore I want to focus on behaviours, not the minutia of data protection law, hoping that as a result, this guidance will remain relevant for longer.

This approach also helps me make these letters more relevant to DPOs that work outside Europe. Not all DPOs operate within the legal environment that is determined by the GDPR, despite the intention of many European politicians that the GDPR should influence the development of the data protection laws of non-European countries.

Turning to the DPOs that do operate within Europe (and those who work for organisations that are not headquartered in Europe but where a part of their organisation's data processing activities falls within the scope of the GDPR), this approach also means that I don't need to spend much time explaining just how local data protection laws vary, despite the existence of the GDPR. That is the task of other commentators.

I should explain at the outset that while I'm an advocate of robust privacy laws which protect individuals from being harmed as a result of the inappropriate use of their personal data, I'm not a fan of the GDPR. It was introduced with an initial aim of harmonising as well as strengthening the existing data protection laws across the European Union. It was designed to replace a European Data Protection Directive which had been in force since 1995, when

Member States had a wide margin of appreciation about how (and the extent to which) the Directive's requirements were expressed in local laws.

During the extensive negotiations prior to the GDPR's implementation, it became very apparent that the member states were not aligned in all areas. The governments, the data protection supervisory authorities, the politicians and the key opinion formers within each Member State did not and have never shared a common view on how personal data should be protected. I'm not going to explain the procedure that is followed when legislative proposals are turned into an EU regulation, all you need to know for the purposes of these letters is that it's a tedious and complicated affair which requires different sets of parties to participate in negotiations, which are sometimes conducted in public and, when the going gets really tough, they continue, and key decision are taken, in private. This way, individuals can't be identified - and so be held accountable - for the consequences of their decisions.

Mistakes are often made when policy decisions are taken in a hurry, and this was certainly the case with the GDPR. To avoid the prospect of many months of parliamentary time being wasted should the draft legislative proposals have to be dropped because agreement had not been reached before European parliamentarians had to face re-election to the European Parliament, the European Commission imposed a deadline on all parties to reach an agreement on the text of a draft Regulation by the end of 2015. A decision needed to be made on: (1) whether it would be preferable to stop working on the proposals; or alternatively (2) to identify what could be agreed, drive the legislation through the European institutions so that it became European law and park the issues where agreement could not be reached.

It was decided that it would be better to agree on something rather than to do nothing. So, to meet this deadline, many issues were parked. Extensive derogations were incorporated into the text, giving Member States the power to override about one third of the Articles that prescribe obligations and requirements. They included some of the key provisions, such as age restrictions relating to children and requirements on how data controllers in the public sector should manage personal data. The local laws that were later passed by each Member State reflected the extensive powers that were given to them to develop standards that reflected local requirements and ensured that the GDPR heroically failed in its mission to harmonise data protection laws throughout Europe.

Some sectors, such as law enforcement and national security, were never designed to fall within the scope of the GDPR. A separate EU regulation applies to personal data processed for law enforcement purposes, while a different set of local laws and practices regulate the processing of personal data for national security purposes. What Europe has ended up with is a patchwork of different data protection standards – and when the standards are set by the GDPR, they are extremely prescriptive in their nature. Those that drafted (and ultimately voted for) the GDPR decided on German-style precision. It wasn't designed to be used by those that prefer pragmatism to dogmatism.

When Professor Lee Bygrave, Director of the Norwegian Research Centre for Computers and Law at the University of Oslo was asked by the International Association of Privacy Processionals for his views on the GDPR to commemorate the second anniversary of its coming into force, he didn't mince his words:

EU Data Protection law — with the EU General Data Protection Regulation in the "front seat" — has taken what I call a "Byzantine turn." By this, I mean three trends. First, the EU data protection system has become an empire in itself and unto itself. Consider its mammoth number of rules, immense officialdom, constitutional standing and strengthened sanctions regime, combined with high-profile judicial support for its cause — all these factors combined give the system the pondus of "empire." With that pondus there comes a certain swagger that bespeaks the following message to the world: "I am now so big that I don't need to justify my being. I am what I am, and I am here to stay, regardless of what you might think." It is not difficult to read this sort of message into the subtext of the GDPR or into the subtext of some of the Court of Justice of the European Union's landmark judgments in this field (e.g., its judgment in "Schrems I"). Of course, such a message is far from unique for EU data protection law; numerous other laws, especially those embodying a nation state's ordre public convey a similar message.

The second dimension to the Byzantine turn is the evermore self-referential thrust of the EU data protection system. It is a system increasingly turned in on itself. Large parts of it are essentially engaged in a conversation with other parts of it. The GDPR exemplifies this well. Many of its provisions are addressed not really to the world-at-large, but also to "insiders." For instance, over one-quarter of the words making up the GDPR's operative provisions are devoted to the workings of supervisory authorities and the European Data Protection Board. At the same time, general discourse on data protection has become extremely GDPR-centric; the regulation has effectively created a vortex that sucks policy discussion into its fold. This is occurring not just in Europe, but also across the globe.

The third aspect of the Byzantine turn concerns the procedural intricacy of the EU data protection regime. Data protection law in general has always had a predominantly procedural thrust. Under the GDPR, however, procedural intricacy has become extreme — and extremely problematic. The GDPR's provisions on the "consistency mechanism" are a case in point. It is often said that the "devil is in the detail," yet excess of detail is in itself a devil. It becomes even more devilish when the detail is set out in cumbersome, dense and arcane prose.

All up, the EU data protection system has become a huge sprawling structure — a Kafkaesque castle full of semantic mazes, winding procedural alleys, subterranean cross-passages and conceptual echo chambers.

I appreciate that the GDPR must be more exhaustive than the directive it replaced if it is to ensure greater pan-European uniformity of rules. Yet, there are costs in trying to leave no stone unturned, just as there is a point where the perfect becomes the enemy of the good.[i]

These are strong comments and I respect Professor Bygrave for his candour. There aren't many academics who have criticised the GDPR in such strident terms. It's not only enlightened UK Data Protection Officers that are convinced that the Regulation should change. German MEP Axel Vosss also concerned about the GDPR's numerous shortcomings, how it has created much legal and practical chaos, how it has led to a compliance costs explosion and how it severely hampers Europe's digital transformation. In the introduction to his paper on fixing the GDPR, Voss explained why a new mindset is needed to uphold robust privacy standards:

The promises of the General Data Protection Regulation (GDPR) are manifold. It is supposed to protect privacy and guarantee the self-determination of the individual. It is supposed to put digital gatekeepers in their place. It is supposed to be a bulwark against the surveillance state and surveillance capitalism. The law is - for its advocates - the new gold standard for data protection. If you are trying to make an honest assessment of the GDPR three years after its application, you will however also hear very different views. Many citizens, research institutes, charitable organisations and small companies strongly complain about yet another EU bureaucracy monster that overcomplicates their daily lives and massively increases their expenses, being out of all proportion in terms of a cost-benefit ratio. Moreover, you will notice well-founded criticism based on fundamental rights, claiming the GDPR to have a detrimental effect on civil liberties and to undermine important standards of the rule of law.

When I wrote the 2011 own-initiative report for a 'Comprehensive approach on personal data protection in the EU' (that resulted in the subsequent GDPR) as Rapporteur of the European Parliament, I was a strong proponent for legislative action. Alarmed by constant data protection scandals, I saw it as our democratic duty to harmonise the fragmented national systems and to strengthen our citizens' right to privacy substantially. In this sense, I would still consider the GDPR a success. However, already during the political negotiations on the GDPR as Shadow Rapporteur, I realized that the law also has numerous shortcomings. Over time, I became more and more critical towards those points and eventually, most of my criticism was confirmed in the public outcry after the GDPR's application in 2018. The European Union did create a law that might be excellent in theory and which did improve the standards for data protection in many areas. Yet, it has also caused legal and practical chaos in other areas.

No matter how good the intentions of the legislators are, their laws will never be perfect. Miscalculations are part of policy-making and we are responsible for fixing them. What shocked me was therefore the reactions of certain decision-makers in Brussels and of data protection authorities, which are disregarding the public outcry until today and which are still unwilling to acknowledge that problems exist. To them, the GDPR is "the perfect law" or even "the privacy bible". To them, existing problems are solely the fault of the Member States that wrongly implement the law; of our companies and citizens, who do not understand it correctly; of the legal advisors, who do not explain it properly; of the supervisory authorities, who do not enforce it properly; and of the opponents of the law, who deliberately create confusion.

After hearing the same line of argumentation again in the LIBE-committee earlier this year, when I was negotiating the new GDPR-resolution as Shadow Rapporteur, I decided to try something new. On 16 February 2021, I launched my own public consultation to hear your thoughts about the GDPR. With more than 180 replies, you reinforced my doubts and described how the GDPR is leading to numerous problems in your daily life. Striking was that only 1/3 of the replies was coming from companies and business associations, while the large majority was from citizens, researchers, scientists, nurses, data protection officers, lawyers, non-profit associations, sport clubs and many more. The following list categorises and summarises your feedback.

While this list concentrates solely on conceptual flaws, legal gaps and practical problems that occurred since the GDPR became effective in 2018, this document does not argue that the law itself should be withdrawn or that its adoption was per se a mistake. Data protection is and must always remain an essential element of our democratic system. Moreover, the GDPR stands for a major improvement of the right to privacy. Neither I nor other critics want to lower the EU's high data protection standards. However, what the list is clearly demonstrating is that the law, in its current form, at the same time abridges other fundamental rights, leads to a compliance costs explosion and severely hampers Europe's digital transformation. We owe it to our citizens to acknowledge these facts and to start fixing the GDPR-related problems through legal adjustments as well as better guidance. What we need is a new mindset when it comes to the use of data. In our digital world, data offers various chances to improve the living standards and to address current problems such as climate change or a pandemic. Only at the second step, we should focus on the risks and build up effective safeguards to prevent potential misuse. Digitalisation is a huge chance for the EU. Let us start by making the GDPR a more balanced law.[ii]

I should also explain that these letters will not spend much time explaining what personal data is and what specific types of information fall outside the scope of local data protection laws. Just think of information as lying on a continuum – with personal data at one end, pseudonymous data in the middle and anonymous data, which falls outside the scope of data protection laws, at the other end. But where should you draw the line and, more importantly, does it really matter?

Don't spend too much time trying to draw the line between pseudonymous and anonymous data. The GDPR defines anonymous data as data that *does not relate to an identified or identifiable natural person or to personal data rendered anonymous so the data subject is not or no longer identifiable.[iii]* From a compliance standpoint, anonymous data makes your life easier. However, even though European data protection supervisory authorities have publicly talked about anonymization for decades, they have not reached a common view on what anonymization means in practice. If you're really interested, Spain's DPA, the Agencia Española de Protección de Datos, and the European Data Protection Supervisor released a joint document in July 2021[iv] entitled '10 Misunderstandings Related to Anonymization'. In the UK, the Information Commissioner's Office consulted stakeholders in May 2021[v] on revisions to its anonymization guidance, an initiative designed to update its previous guidance, published as a 2012 code of practice on "Anonymization:

managing data protection risk". Read those documents and ask yourself whether you have really learnt anything new.

For those that need to understand the key anonymization / pseudonymization issues, data protection lawyers Andrew Burt, Alfred Rossi & Sophie Stalla-Bourdillon have summarised them as follows:

In 2007 the Article 29 Working party issued an opinion that articulated the difference between "anonymization" and "pseudonymization."[vi] The main difference between the two defined pseudonymization as privacy protective and technically reversible. On the other hand, anonymization was defined as such: "Disguising identities can also be done in a way that no reidentification is possible, e.g. by one-way cryptography, which creates in general anonymized data."

The 2007 opinion explained that if "appropriate technical measures" were put in place to prevent reidentification of data, that data can be considered anonymous.

In 2014, the Article 29 Working Party issued opinion on anonymisation techniques. This opinion explained that the difference between anonymization and pseudonymization lays in the likelihood of reidentifiability — whether it's possible to derive personal information from deidentified data.[vii] As study after study has demonstrated, however, it's pretty much impossible to perfectly anonymize data, meaning some possibility of reidentification often remains. The Working Party went further and opined that both aggregation and destruction of the raw data were also needed to achieve anonymization:

"It is critical to understand that when a data controller does not delete the original (identifiable) data at event-level, and the data controller hands over part of this dataset (for example after removal or masking of identifiable data), the resulting dataset is still personal data. Only if the data controller would aggregate the data to a level where the individual events are no longer identifiable, the resulting dataset can be qualified as anonymous."

In other words, only by aggregating data into group statistics and permanently deleting the original data could organisations have full confidence their data was anonymized and therefore outside the scope of data protection regulations in the EU.

Due to this U-turn, EU regulators still vacillate between the 2007 and 2014 standards. Some regulators stated a residual risk of reidentification is acceptable if the right precautions are in place. Regulators like the UK Information Commissioner's Office and Ireland's Data Protection Commission took this track. But other DPAs, like France's Commission Nationale de l'Informatique et des Libertés, used a more absolutist language in their guidance.

Organizations attempting to comply with these standards and aiming to meet EU anonymization requirements get stuck between a rock and a hard place.[viii]

Now, back to my letters. Try not to get too dispirited because a lot of data protection stuff is complicated. Remain positive and ask yourself, when knotty problems arise, what is the common-sense approach to the matter in hand? What is the reasonable behaviour that a responsible organisation should be expected demonstrate? What actions can an organisation's senior management team readily explain and justify to an inquisitive journalist?

In following my advice I do hope, should you have an unfortunate encounter with an aggrieved individual or a concerned privacy regulator, that you will have a credible story to tell to lessen the gravity of your organisation's offence. In explaining what your organisation has done (or has planned to do) to address the relevant privacy risks, a pragmatic regulator might well be minded to exercise forbearance, to allow it the benefit of the doubt and not to immediately embark on any formal enforcement action.

As you read these letters, just remember that my advice needn't always be strictly followed. You, being unconfident, self-conscious, and all-too-aware-of-your-flaws, potentially have as much to contribute to the field of data protection, or the world, as anyone else. If you have a great idea or a cunning plan that will help improve the level of your organisation's compliance with data protection laws, then go for it. Just because I didn't suggest it here doesn't mean it's unlikely to work.

Finally, I just hope that you won't make nearly as many mistakes as I've made in my career. I'm only human, and we all make mistakes. I have tried to learn from my mistakes, though. And, when it's time for you to move on, as I am now moving on, let's hope that your colleagues will appreciate that you tried, at the very least, to be a decent Data Protection Officer.

1 DOING THE RIGHT THING

Congratulations on your appointment. You've either been successful in your application to become a privacy professional, or you've been given some data protection tasks because they needed to be done and no one else in your organisation was either willing or available to do them. That's in the past. Now, you must be keen to understand what it is that this data protection role involves and, most importantly, how you can achieve success in the role.

It's not an easy task to demonstrate success in data protection. Much depends on what it is that you are seeking to achieve, what metrics you are being measured by, and how seriously your organisation takes its data protection obligations. A few organisations appoint DPOs because they want to get data protection right. Others appoint DPOs because they have to.

What matters a lot is perception. The optics of privacy are important because not many people within your organisation are likely have much, let alone a deep, understanding of privacy law and regulation, and you are unlikely to want to feel that all you do every day is challenge your colleagues how they perform their work tasks. I expect that you will want to be given an appropriate amount of respect from your work colleagues. You will want to take on work that is both interesting and demanding. You will also want to achieve something positive during your working day. Decent DPOs need to adopt a positive attitude and cajole their co-workers into adopting good data protection practices.

You may be the first person to be formally appointed as a DPO in your organisation, so in my letter on how to prioritise your work, I'll explain how to start a data protection programme and what responsibilities could be assigned to other staff so that you can focus on the essentials. Keeping on top of developments in the privacy field is essential. You'll often be expected to brief your senior management team on changes to data protection regulations and requirements - and also to update your organisation's IT security and legal teams. In my letter on education, I'll be offering tips on how to keep your privacy knowledge up to date.

As a DPO, you will be expected to help design new products services, develop policies and data protection practices, ensure that the IT security team defines and reviews your organisation's security strategy, as well as be aware of everything else that your organisation does. There's going to be a lot of walking around, or scheduling routine catch-up calls with your colleagues. Decent DPOs are visible to their colleagues. Don't think you can hide away in the corner of an office and expect everyone to come to you. Some – but not all – of these obligations will be covered in these letters. Advising on how to prepare for every single aspect of the life of a DPO would make these letters much too long and dull. Instead, I'll assume that you know where to go to get the additional technical support you'll need to better understand and address your organisation's data protection obligations.

You're not going to be able to convince others that you are good at your job if you are not personally confident that you both know what is expected of you as a privacy professional and that you have the mindset which will enable you to focus on the key tasks. You will probably need to remind others that some of the responsibilities they may try to allocate to you are not those that any privacy professional, or a privacy professional with your amount of experience, should undertake. Former Information Commissioner Richard Thomas was always ready to remind those who criticised his office for inaction that his team had to be selective to be effective. Future historians will judge whether the correct calls were made during his time in charge. And your successors will judge how you performed, too.

Measuring your success

Success comes in many forms. You may be recognised by your peers for being outspoken on data protection issues. You may appear on conference platforms or Twitter feeds and be regarded as someone with something worthwhile to say. Or, you may be recognised by your organisation's internal audit team for leading a function that hasn't failed an audit. You may even be quietly consulted by officials working for your national data protection supervisory authority who are keen to understand whether the advice they publish is capable of being followed by the organisations they regulate.

The trouble with a career in data protection compliance is that it's quite a lonely job. People who work in data protection compliance teams don't often make many friends in, say, the marketing teams. But before you start to worry about how popular you are, first, you must appreciate what the law requires a Data Protection Officer to do. Then, you should appreciate what additional tasks your organisation expects you to do, in order that you can decide whether you, or other members of your team, have the time and / or the resources to carry them out, and that you would not be conflicted by carrying them out.

Data protection trainer Tim Turner has explained[ix] that your primary role is giving advice on data protection issues. As far as your organisation is concerned, you are the expert on the legislation and how applies to whatever your organisation does. You will be required advise what to do when it receives a Subject Access Request, when the police want information in relation to a crime, and whether it needs to notify the ICO or the affected individuals about a data protection incident. You must be available to anyone (within reason) and you must be capable of thinking on the spot.

You will also monitor your organisation's compliance – not with just privacy law itself, but with other relevant legislation. You will monitor compliance with your organisation's internal policies and procedures. You will be the person the organisation trusts with access to its premises, records and staff. The relationship between you and your organisation is ongoing and the bond of trust should deepen with time. But earning the trust of your co-workers takes time. If you are in it for the short term, you're going to find it hard to make your mark.

You are not a project manager, nor a change manager. You might well need someone with transformational change or project management skills to support you, but you will primarily have an advice-giving, monitoring role. If you're the type of person that is only focused on setting up structures and processes, you're probably not the right person to be the DPO.

As a DPO, your success will be measured with a range of metrics. Organisations must generally respond to Subject Access Requests within a month and notify significant personal data breaches to supervisory authorities within days. Data protection supervisory authorities monitor complaints relating to the late delivery of Subject Access Requests, while your personal data breach reports will have to include, when appropriate, an explanation for any reporting delays. You will try to protect your organisation from any enforcement action that the supervisory authority might be minded to take if the statutory deadlines are continually missed. In this context, success is measured in terms of the absence of any enforcement action.

Project teams may expect you or, if you have them, other experienced members of your privacy team to carry out Data Protection Impact Assessments within extremely short time constraints. They may be unhappy with the requests for additional information that you or your colleagues will make, or with the recommendations that will be made in light of the information that has been disclosed. In this context, success will be measured in terms of the impression you leave with the project team that the impact assessment has been a worthwhile exercise, not just a form filling chore where no benefit has been derived.

You may also be required, at virtually no notice, to develop briefing material in response to requests from members of your senior management team or from other colleagues on any privacy issue. In this context, success will be measured in terms of your ability to hit key deadlines and to explain matters using language and the level of detail that the requesting party requires. The recipients of your advice may well have no idea about the effort it took to ensure that appropriate advice was provided in a timely manner, so you should not be surprised if they don't show much gratitude. Some recipients, however, will be delighted at the way in which you have engaged with them, and you should ensure that this positive feedback is reflected in your next performance appraisal.

Some DPOs want to make a real impact in the privacy world. Others simply want to earn a living. There's nothing wrong with either approach. You should not feel obliged to be passionate about privacy. It's your job to act in a professional manner. It's not your job to robustly defend your organisation from those who have a good reason to criticise it. You can leave that task to your organisation's complaints team.

Engaging consultants & privacy tech vendors

If your organisation instructs a firm of data protection consultants, you must appreciate that their goals may be different to yours. Their goals are likely to be measured in metrics that reflect the billable hours that will be charged. It's all about money. A consultant exists to be farmed out to any client that needs and can afford help, perhaps privacy knowledge transfer into the organisation, or perhaps writing reports when their client (i.e. your organisation) lacks the internal resources and/or the knowhow to do this work themselves. A consultant may be engaged to help provide assurance that any advice your organisation has previously obtained, perhaps from you from or the in-house legal team, is sufficiently robust. Or, consultants may be engaged to provide assurance that the privacy controls that your organisation has (or should have) are in place and are working effectively.

The UK's largest professional services firms have recently received a considerable amount of adverse publicity regarding poor audits and are currently trying to ringfence their audit practices from their consulting arms. They are under mounting pressure from regulators to eliminate the potential conflicts of interest that arise when there is a risk that asking too many difficult questions could result in the loss of other lucrative consulting contracts.

There is a subtle difference between the provision of advice and the more formal assurance / audit work. A data protection audit may well involve a much more rigorous, evidence based, inspection of your organisation's practices. The results are likely to be reported to your organisation's audit committee, and consequently the auditor's follow up recommendations are likely to be tracked by your senior management team until they have all been addressed. Many organisations steer clear of requiring formal data protection audits, and opt for data protection healthchecks, which are much more informal and where the results don't need to be reported to audit committees.

Decent data protection consultants will help explain from an objective, evidence-based perspective, how well (or, more likely, how poorly) your organisation's existing systems and processes meet legal and regulatory expectations. They might also suggest how new systems and processes could be put in place to achieve a higher level of compliance with privacy laws, regulations and regulatory expectations.

When they perform their work, you should bear in mind that their primary duty is to their employer, not to their client. They will therefore carry out their work through the prism of their employer's risk profile unless they are specifically instructed to use the organisation's risk profile. Consultants working for clients in the more heavily regulated industries, such as financial services and telecommunications, will be expected to explain what 'good' practice is, or what 'best' practice means, and how far the organisation's practices have deviated from 'best practice' standards. Regulators will expect to be informed of audit fails. Consultants working for clients in the less heavily regulated industries, such as retail and estate agencies, may simply be asked to explain just what practices they can get away with.

Consultants employed by the large professional services firms are likely to rely heavily on standard data protection methodologies and template reports that their employers have used many times before. Well-managed consulting firms have created comprehensive libraries of standard health check questions and controls. Their written reports are likely to draw from templates of comments that can be used time and time again.

The smaller professional services firms may well use a different business model. These firms may not have had the resources to create well-developed libraries of data protection questions and controls. They may hire in (or subcontract work to) independent professional consultants who will work for the firm on an as-required basis. They may rebadge the independent consultant's work as the firm's own. In terms of quality control, these firms may struggle to offer their clients a consistent service. This is because the quality of their service will depend to a much greater extent on the calibre of the independent consultant that was employed for that engagement; whether the methodology used to supply the service was the intellectual property of the firm or the independent consultant; and whether that methodology could be competently replicated by other independent consultants.

When you ask a professional services firm "what can you do for me?", you should accept that the answer will depend on what services they feel they can sell you. I once asked a consultant whether he felt he had sufficient expertise to carry out a particular task, he quietly replied that it didn't really matter: "In the land of the bind, the one-eyed man is king." But it does matter. If the consulting firm does not have readily available professionals with the capacity and skillsets to provide the services your organisation really requires, a range of ethical issues will arise. These firms should not promise to provide a service that they are not confident of delivering. Sometimes, this happens. Some firms, when pitching to clients, include in their proposal packs the CVs of experienced staff they know probably won't be available to carry out the client's engagement should the bid be accepted. They hope that the client won't mind if the staff that carry out the fieldwork aren't those whose CVs were initially presented.

You should ensure that your organisation agrees detailed Statements of Work with the consultants they engage, and that these agreements specify who will be carrying out and who will be supervising the work. If these details are vague, there is a risk that the consulting firm will assign people that don't have the appropriate level of experience for the project. Decent consultants ought to explain to their employers, and their client (i.e. your organisation) the risks involved in them being expected to complete work for which they lack the relevant experience. Some consultants don't do this. They may work on that project, regardless of whether they are appropriately supervised.

Any decent consultant's CV must evidence that they have previously conducted data protection audits and healthchecks, data protection impact assessments, created Records of Processing Activities and advised organisations on the actions it should take following a personal data breach. Decent DPOs ask for additional evidence of a consultant's practical experience in these areas if their CV doesn't mention them. Assess the amount of experience they have, and whether the sectors they have worked in are like the sector your own organisation is in. You will want to work with consultants that share the culture of your organisation, and that will be most easily achieved if the consultant has demonstrable experience in your sector. The best DPOs find consultants they trust and will continue to work with as their careers develop.

As a DPO, you'll be frequently contacted by a large range of privacy tech vendors, each of which will be striving to demonstrate the value their products deliver. Some vendors will claim they help organisations find and understand the data they have, compare it against applicable global laws and regulations, and remediate any gaps in compliance. Other vendors will show you research which claims that large percentages of consumers around the world would feel more reassured and would be more likely to spend with companies that were officially certified to data privacy standards they can help your organisation obtain.

It's important for organisations that use data to do so ethically and in compliance with the law, but those are not the only reasons why the privacy tech sector is booming. Some privacy tech vendors claim that companies with exceptional privacy operations gain a competitive advantage, strengthen customer relationships, and accelerate sales. I haven't seen much empirical evidence to support this contention.

According to a report by the Privacy Tech Alliance and the Future of Privacy Forum published in June 2021, regulations are often the biggest driver for buyers' initial privacy tech purchases. Organisations serving global markets increasingly need to buy privacy tech that offers data availability and control and supports its utility, in addition to regulatory compliance. Evidently:

- *buyers favour integrated solutions over one-off solutions;*
- *collaborations, partners, cross-selling, and joint ventures between privacy tech vendors are increasing to provide buyers with integrated suites of services and attract additional market share;*
- *private equity and private equity-backed companies will continue their "roll-up" strategies of buying niche providers to build a package of companies to provide the integrated solutions buyer's favour;*
- *venture capital will continue funding the privacy tech sector, though not every seller has the same level of success fundraising;*
- *big companies may acquire strategically valuable, niche players;*
- *small start-ups may experience of struggle to gain market traction absent a truly novel or superb solution; and*
- *buyers will face challenges in future-proofing their privacy strategies.*[x]

Without doubt, the privacy tech market is evolving and is rapidly becoming more sophisticated. Whether the products on offer meet the needs of most organisations is another matter. The trends are clear, however – as with other areas of the internet, the larger providers dominate the market, buying up smaller competitors and reducing the real choice available to organisations that need to buy privacy tech.

Taking external legal advice

Over time, your knowledge of data protection laws as they apply to your sector may well become much deeper than that held by members of your organisation's legal team, or even deeper than that held by the external lawyers that your organisation engages. As a DPO, you will be separated from your organisation's legal team, you (most likely) won't report to the General Counsel, nor will you hold a current legal practicing certificate. Do not assume that any advice you may give to your organisation will be legal advice covered by legal privilege. Be careful how you respond should your data protection supervisory authority ask for any documents in relation to an investigation they are running. It is your job to be as open as you can with the supervisory authorities. You will therefore be conflicted if you feel obliged to divulge advice you have previously given to your organisation when the organisation had previously assumed that the advice had been given confidence.

If your organisation requires legal advice that can be protected from being disclosed to a data protection supervisory authority because it is subject to 'legal professional privilege', you must ensure that the advice is provided by someone other than yourself. You may get to read the information, but this is not the same as being under a duty to disclose it.

Be wary of dealing with in-house lawyers who paste phrases like 'subject to legal professional privilege' in the header or footer of every email they send. Organisations can't prevent documents from being disclosed just by ensuring that a particular phrase is used to protect it. Much depends on the context within which the communication was sent and what instructions were given to the lawyers.

Legal professional privilege is the rule of evidence that entitles a party to withhold certain confidential documents from inspection in a discovery process or for use in evidence even if they are relevant. There are two forms of legal professional privilege, legal advice privilege and litigation privilege.

Confidential information contained in communications between a lawyer and their client can only benefit from the protection of legal advice privilege where that confidential communication is for the purpose of seeking, giving or receiving legal advice. DPOs cannot be expected to provide legal advice.

Where litigation privilege is claimed over communications made prior to the commencement of litigation or other sufficiently adversarial proceedings then there must have been at least a reasonable likelihood of that litigation or those other proceedings taking place. A mere possibility they may take place will not be sufficient.

Often, an inquiry made to an external lawyer can result in advice being provided to your data protection supervisory authority, only a part of which is protected by litigation privilege. Much depends on the subject matter of the investigation and the way the investigation is carried out. If an investigation or inquiry moves from a fact gathering phase to a subsequent more confrontational phase then it may be the case that litigation privilege can apply to the later phase of the process.

In the event of enforcement action being taken against your organisation, you may be asked by your supervisory authority to disclose any legal advice that has been received. Adopting an adversarial approach and refusing to help your supervisory authority's investigation may be considered an aggravating factor when the authority determines what penalty should be imposed on your organisation. As DPO, you will probably want to work closely with the supervisory authority, deploying whatever soft skills you have. You will probably want to charm them and reassure them that you are just as concerned about the matter in hand as they are. Alternatively, you may work for organisation that prefers to adopt a more confrontational approach, particularly if the authority's investigation relates to a new and innovative technology or process. If this is the case, then your organisation's legal team had better out gun the authority's legal team, as the cost of failure can be high.

Passion and privacy

I've already told you that you don't have to be passionate about privacy to be a decent Data Protection Officer. You don't need be a privacy evangelist, although many DPOs start off this way. Let's be clear about what you are not expected to do. It's not necessary for you to adopt anything like the crusading approach that was vividly described by the Victorian poet Sir Henry Newbolt:

> *To set the cause above renown,*
> *To love the game beyond the prize,*
> *To honour, while you strike him down,*
> *The foe that comes with fearless eyes;*
> *To count the life of battle good,*
> *And dear the land that gave you birth,*
> *And dearer yet the brotherhood*
> *That binds the brave of all the earth.*[xi]

The data protection brotherhood isn't like Camelot. The UK's Information Commissioner isn't King Arthur. Nor is the Chairman of the European Data Protection Board, and neither is the European Data Protection Supervisor. You are not one of the King's privacy knights, charged with seeking out and safeguarding all the secrets that are held in that holy crystal chalice of private words and thoughts. Privacy is not a game. Nor is it a war. It's not necessary for you to lead your organisation in an all-out attack against your data protection supervisory authority. A privacy win for you is not necessarily a privacy loss to them.

You may well work for a data driven organisation, one with strong leaders whose aims are to increase profits year on year. But so what? I review my investments each month with one purpose – to see whether they have increased in value. I don't review them to assess whether my money is invested in companies that are respectful of individual's data protection rights. You, however, will have your own views about what data protection behaviours are appropriate and lawful. You are entitled to act as any reasonable DPO would see fit. Sir Henry's poem, championing the virtues of chivalry and sportsmanship, was inspired by the memorials in the Chapel of Clifton School in Bristol that commemorated former pupils who had died by accident or disease serving the British Empire. Those days have passed. No one expects you to die - or even to get ill - while serving the interests of data protection.

Even if your organisation is established in the UK, you don't need to follow the dogma which professes that data protection rights, having been elevated by European law to the level of a fundamental human right, automatically trumps all other human rights. The rigid European legal codes give European citizens legal rights only when the laws specify how these rights can be exercised and can be very challenging for most people to comprehend. Your duty is to think in wider terms. In the words of retired High Court Judge Harry Ognall:

Looking at the European emphasis on human rights leads me to the following conclusion. No citizen within these shores has ever needed or sought to have his human rights defined or constrained by any definition of human rights. Our rights are limitless, unless prohibited. They are presumed, not defined. The yeoman of England stands tall, arms akimbo, and says, 'Show me where it says I can't.[xii]

Your role as your organisation's DPO won't last for ever, but there's no reason you not to enjoy a reasonably fulfilled life as you carry out your duties. Remember psychologist Oliver Burkeman's eight secrets to fulfilment:

There will always be too much to do – and this realisation is liberating. *There's no reason to assume that there is any fit between the demands on your time – all the things you would like to do or feel you ought to* *do – and the amount of time available. The demands will keep increasing, while your capacities will remain largely fixed. It follows that any attempt to "get on top of everything" is doomed. Indeed, it's worse than that – the more tasks you get done, the more tasks you'll generate.*

The upside is that you needn't berate yourself for failing to do it all, since doing it all is impossible. The only viable solution is to make a shift: from a life spent trying not to neglect anything, to one spent proactively and consciously choosing what to neglect, in favour of what matters most. I say more about this in my letters on priorities and overwhelming workloads.

When stumped by a life choice, choose "enlargement" over happiness. *Major personal decisions should be made not by asking "Will this make me happy?" but "Will this choice enlarge me or diminish me?" We're terrible at predicting what will make us happy: the question swiftly gets bogged down in our narrow preferences for security and control. But the enlargement question elicits a deeper, intuitive response. You tend to just know whether, say, leaving or remaining in a job, though it might bring short-term comfort, would mean cheating yourself of growth. I'll say more about this in my letter on never giving up.*

The capacity to tolerate minor discomfort is a superpower. *It's shocking to realise how readily we set aside even our greatest ambitions in life, merely to avoid easily tolerable levels of unpleasantness. You already know it won't kill you to endure the mild agitation of getting back to work on an important project; initiating a difficult conversation with a colleague; or checking your whether colleagues have done what they said they would get done – but you can waste years in avoidance, nonetheless.*

It's possible, instead, to make a game of gradually increasing your capacity for discomfort, like weight training at the gym. When you expect that an action will be accompanied by feelings of irritability, anxiety or boredom, it's usually possible to let that feeling arise and fade, while doing the action anyway. The rewards come so quickly, in terms of what you'll accomplish, that it soon becomes the more appealing way to live.

The advice you don't want to hear is usually the advice you need. *It isn't fun to confront whatever emotional experiences you're avoiding – if it were, you wouldn't avoid them – so the advice that could really help is advice that is likely to make you uncomfortable. You may need to introspect with care here, since bad advice from manipulative colleagues at work is also likely to make you uncomfortable.*

The future will never provide the reassurance you seek from it. *As the ancient Greek and Roman stoics understood, much of our suffering arises from attempting to control what is not in our control. And the main thing we try but fail to control – the seasoned worriers among us, anyway – is the future. We want to know, from our vantage point in the present, that things will be OK later. But we never can.*

It's freeing to grasp that no amount of fretting will ever alter this truth. It's still useful to make plans. But do that with the awareness that a plan is only ever a present-moment statement of intent, not a lasso thrown around the future to bring it under control. The spiritual teacher Jiddu Krishnamurti said his secret was simple: "I don't mind what happens." That needn't mean not trying to make life better, for yourself or others. It just means not living each day anxiously braced to see if things work out as you hoped. I'll say more about this in my letter on accepting risks.

The solution to imposter syndrome is to see that you are one. *When Oliver Burkeman first wrote about how useful it is to remember that everyone is totally just winging it, all the time, we hadn't yet entered the current era of leaderly incompetence (Brexit, Trump, coronavirus). Now, it's harder to ignore. But the lesson to be drawn isn't that we're doomed to chaos. It's that you – unconfident, self-conscious, all-too-aware-of-your-flaws – potentially have as much to contribute to your field, or the world of data protection, as anyone else.*

Humanity is divided into two: on the one hand, those who are improvising their way through life, patching solutions together and putting out fires as they go, but deluding themselves otherwise; and on the other, those doing the same, except that they know it. It's infinitely better to be the latter (although too much "assertiveness training" consists of techniques for turning yourself into the former).

Remember: the reason you can't hear other people's inner monologues of self-doubt isn't that they don't have them. It's that you only have access to your own mind.

Selflessness is overrated. *Respectable people are raised to think a life well spent means helping others – and plenty of self-help gurus stand ready to affirm that kindness, generosity and volunteering are the route to happiness. There's truth here, but it generally gets tangled up with deep-seated issues of guilt and self-esteem.*

If you're prone to thinking you should be helping more, that's probably a sign that you could afford to direct more energy to your own idiosyncratic ambitions and enthusiasms. As the Buddhist teacher Sisan Piver observed, it's radical, at least for some of us, to ask how we'd enjoy spending an hour or day of discretionary time. And the irony is that you don't serve anyone else by suppressing your true passions anyway. Often, by doing your thing – as opposed to what you think you ought to be doing – you kindle a fire that helps keep the rest of us warm. I'll say more about this in my letter on open mindedness.

Know when to move on. *Finally, it's necessary to know when something that's meant a great deal to you has reached its natural endpoint, and that the most creative choice would be to turn to what's next.* I'll say more about this in my letter on never giving up. [xiii]

17

2 APPLYING THE KEY DATA PROTECTION PRINCIPLES

Most organisations process a lot of personal data for a wide range of purposes, and it is almost impossible for lawmakers to develop a prescriptive set of rules that can cater for every eventuality. However, it's not necessary for laws to be developed that cater for every eventuality. The more forward-looking countries have developed laws that focus on compliance with general data protection principles – and these principles need to be interpreted in light of the specifics of each case. Local laws differ in the level of detail that prescribe how each principle is to be interpreted, what exemptions apply, and what actions organisations should take to fully comply with the principle. A common set of principles has emerged, and these are reflected in the privacy laws that are in place around the world.

Local laws and practices also differ on the extent that each principle is enforced. While the laws infer that each principle is just as important as another principle, in practice the reality is that compliance with some principles are far more important than compliance with others, as a breach of these principles heightens the risk that an individual may be caused harm and distress.

Taking the example set by the EU's General Data Protection Regulation, the key data protection principles are:

Lawfulness, fairness & transparency

This principle consists of three distinctly different elements. 'Lawfulness' relates to compliance with data protection laws and regulations, 'fairness' relates to best practice and a balanced approach in relation to individuals, and 'transparency' relates to informing individuals of the existence of your organisation's processing operations and their purposes.

Lawfulness

Lawfulness means that your organisation's activities must comply with data protection laws and regulations. As a DPO, you must not only know about the Data Protection Act 2018 and the UK GDPR but you must also have *expert knowledge of data protection law and practices*.[xiv] Data protection provisions are scattered across many other laws besides the UK GDPR. They are incorporated, for example, in employment laws, health laws and marketing laws. The proposed use of personal data must, for example, have an appropriate legal basis for the processing to be considered lawful.[xv] The legal bases enable your organisation, for example, to process personal data when the processing is necessary for the performance of a contract with an individual, or when your organisation needs to take steps at the request of the individual prior into entering into a contract. The legal bases also permit your organisation to process personal data when under a legal obligation to do so, or when they have a legitimate interest to do so. I've rarely encountered occasions when decent organisations lacked a proper legal basis to do what they planned to do.

Fairness

Fairness means respecting individuals. For example, this includes not using complicated language to describe your organisation's processing purpose and not deviating from good practice or common practice in a specific area. Fairness also entails not surprising individuals, and, if something may be unexpected, being extra- clear about it. Additionally, the fairness principle means that individuals should be informed if they are required to provide the personal data that is being requested of them and told what the consequences could be if they refused to do so. Finally, your organisation should make individuals aware of the risks that specific processing operations may expose them to.[xvi]

Transparency

Your organisations must provide individuals with all the information that is necessary to enable them to use their rights. The information must be adjusted to the specific circumstances and context of the processing.

Individuals have the right to be informed about the collection and use of their personal data. Local laws differ in prescribing precisely what types of information must be provided, and when. The GDPR sets the gold standard.[xvii] Individuals must be provided with an extensive amount of information including the purposes for processing their personal data, the retention periods for that personal data, and who it will be shared with. It does not matter that the vast majority of individuals will not read the information that is presented to them. Decent DPOs must ensure that for the tiny minority of individuals that are so minded, sufficient information is provided so that they are forewarned.

The long list of information that must be made available to individuals includes:

- the name and contact details of the organisation;
- the name and contact details of its representative;
- the contact details of its data protection officer;
- the purposes of the processing;
- the lawful basis for the processing;
- the legitimate interests for the processing;
- the recipients or categories of recipients of the personal data;
- the details of transfers of the personal data to any third countries or international organisations;
- the retention periods for the personal data;
- the rights available to individuals in respect of the processing;
- the right to withdraw consent;
- the right to lodge a complaint with a supervisory authority;
- the details of whether individuals are under a statutory or contractual obligation to provide the personal data; and
- the details of the existence of automated decision-making, including profiling.

Additionally, if the information is not collected directly from the individual but from other sources, the following details must be provided to the individual:

- the categories of personal data obtained; and
- the source of the personal data.

This information must be provided at the time their personal data is collected from them, or shortly thereafter. If personal data is obtained from other sources, individuals must be provided with privacy information within a reasonable period of obtaining the data and no later than one month.

There are a few circumstances when organisations do not need to provide people with privacy information, such as:

- if an individual already has the information;
- if it would be impossible or would involve a disproportionate effort to provide it to them;
- if providing the information would render impossible or seriously impair the achievement of the objectives of the processing;
- if an organisation is required by law to obtain or disclose the information; or
- if the organisation is subject to an obligation of professional secrecy regulated by a law that covers the personal information.

If your organisation discloses personal information to other organisations, it must

- as part of the privacy information it provides, explain who it is giving their information to, unless it is relying on an exception or an exemption;
- disclose the names of the organisations or the categories that they fall within; choosing the option that is most meaningful; and
- consider, as a matter of good practice, using a dashboard to let people manage who their data is sold to, or shared with, where they have a choice.

If your organisation receives personal information from other organisations, it must

- as part of the privacy information it provides, explain who it is giving their information to, unless it is relying on an exception or an exemption;

- consider carrying out a Data Protection Impact Assessment to find ways to mitigate the risks of the processing if it is considered impossible to provide privacy information to individuals, or if such an exercise would involve a disproportionate effort;
- if the organisation's purpose for using the personal data is different to that for which it was originally obtained, tell people about this, as well as what its lawful basis is for the processing; and
- provide this privacy information within a reasonable period of having obtained the information, and no later than one month.

If your organisation receives personal information from publicly available sources. it must

- still provide people with privacy information unless it is relying on an exception or an exemption;
- consider carrying out a Data Protection Impact Assessment to find ways to mitigate the risks of the processing if it is considered impossible to provide privacy information to individuals, or if such an exercise would involve a disproportionate effort;
- be clear with individuals about any unexpected or intrusive uses of personal data, such as combining information about them from several different sources; and
- provide this privacy information within a reasonable period of having obtained the information, and no later than one month.

Organisations that apply any form of Artificial Intelligence to personal information must:

- be upfront about it and explain the purposes for using it;

- if the purposes for using the personal information are unclear at the outset, individuals should still be given an indication of how their information will be used; and
- if AI is used to make solely automated decisions that have legal effects, the privacy notice should explain why this information is relevant and what impact it is going to have on individuals.

I say more about Artificial Intelligence in my letter on accepting risks.

The privacy information your organisation provides must be concise, transparent, intelligible, easily accessible, and must also be in plain language.[xviii] This is a hugely problematic requirement, as many organisations have complex processing operations which are very hard to set out in an intelligible manner, let alone concisely. Don't be tempted to use privacy notices that have been written by lawyers using legal language, as it can be hard for ordinary members of the public to understand this information. I apply the "would my mum understand this stuff" test. If I think she wouldn't, I try to rewrite it, even though I can't think of any time she would ever want to read it. Never was the proverb so apt: "you can lead a horse to water, but you can't make it drink."

Data protection supervisory authorities consider that it is often most effective to provide privacy information to people using a combination of different techniques such as layering, dashboards, icons and just-in-time notices. They consider that user testing is also a good way to get feedback on how effective the delivery of privacy information is. Whatever methods I've tried, from the complaints letters I've received I realise that I've mostly failed to engage customers sufficiently to feel confident that they know how my organisation processes their personal data.

Data protection supervisory authorities also expect your

organisation to regularly review, and where necessary, update the privacy information. Any new uses of an individual's personal data must be brought to their attention before the processing starts, and they may be required to consent to new uses. I say more about this issue in my comments on purpose limitation.

With apologies for repeating myself, my experience is that most of the time, the only people that read privacy notices are those that are paid to read privacy notices. I've been a privacy pro for over 30 years, yet I hardly ever read even the ones that apply to me. I, along with surely most other people, have no more time or desire to know about what an organisation does with my personal data than I care about the internal workings of a car engine. I need to know what type of fuel my car uses, but I'm not interested in knowing much more about the engine works or precisely what information the car discloses, nor to whom, should it be involved in an accident. Getting the balance right between providing sufficient information but not so much as to overwhelm the reader to the extent that they stop reading the privacy notice is hard.

Data protection supervisory authorities generally wait until they receive a complaint before investigating whether sufficient information appears in a privacy notice. They can then decide whether the advice they've published has been followed and take enforcement action when they consider it has not.

Data protection supervisory authorities also cover themselves by explaining to organisations that, when telling individuals who your organisation is giving their information to, it is good practice to list either the names of the recipient organisations or the categories they fall into, depending on which option is the most meaningful. Depending on the authority, getting the right to be informed wrong can leave organisations open to fines and it can lead to reputational damage. In October 2020, the ICO took enforcement action against the credit provider Experian for an insufficiently detailed privacy notice.[xix] An investigation had revealed that UK Credit Reference Agencies were trading, enriching and enhancing people's personal data without their knowledge. This processing resulted in Experian developing products which were used by commercial organisations, political parties or charities to find new customers, identify the people most likely to be able to afford goods and services, and build profiles about people. The ICO found that significant 'invisible' processing took place, likely affecting millions of adults in the UK. It was 'invisible' because the individual was not aware that the organisation is collecting and using their personal data. Experian was required to change its practices, but it wasn't fined.

Experian got off lightly.

In September 2021, the Irish Data Protection Commission (DPC) announced a decision to fine WhatsApp €225 million. The DPC concluded that WhatsApp had failed to provide required privacy information to WhatsApp users; had failed to provide privacy information to the contacts of WhatsApp users — "non-users" — whose personal data was processed in order to show users which of their contacts were also WhatsApp users; had failed to make privacy information available in an easily accessible form; and had also failed to comply with the overarching transparency principle. The DPC required WhatsApp to provide the required privacy information within the three months of the date of the decision and issued a reprimand.

It took the DPC a long time to announce this decision. As WhatsApp's processing of personal data substantially affects data subjects in more than one EU Member State and their sole establishment in the EU was in Ireland, the cooperation and consistency provisions under the GDPR (the one-stop shop provision) were triggered. To comply with these provisions, the DPC submitted a draft decision to all other EU data protection supervisory authorities. Six authorities commented on the decision;

six authorities submitted relevant and reasoned objections (France's data protection authority doing both; the federal German authority objected and the supervisory authorities for two Laender were also involved). It was not possible for the DPC to reach a consensus with these authorities on a number of points, so these were submitted to the European Data Protection Board for it to reach a decision under Article 65. In a number of places, the decision incorporates the conclusions of the EDPB.

Data protection lawyer Ruth Boardman commented: *the decision establishes that privacy notices must be detailed – with far more detail being given than is currently typically the case – and must be easily accessible, without use of multiple linked documents, which may be hard to find and assimilate. The decision also incorporates findings of the EDPB on how fines should be calculated.*

WhatsApp stated that it will appeal the decision.

Easily accessible privacy information – take care with multiple linked documents

GDPR Article 12(1) provides that information provided to a data subject has to be "easily accessible." Information contained in multiple, linked documents is not always easily accessible – especially where the documents contain overlapping, but slightly different, information. The decision notes: "The user should not have to work hard to access the prescribed information; nor should he/she be left wondering if he/she has exhausted all available sources of information and nor should he/she have to try to reconcile discrepancies between the various pieces of information set out in different locations."

The decision does not stop use of linked documents. In some circumstances, we think there may be good reasons for using this technique. However, controllers must ensure there is an easy way for a data subject to know they have seen all relevant information (such as also having a composite notice) and must avoid inconsistencies between documents.

The decision notes that, in the course of the investigation, WhatsApp had taken steps to address some concerns of the investigator over accessibility of information. Design features to note are:

- *Avoid a continuous scroll of information, with no way for the user to see short-cut options after the home page.*

- *Avoid embedding a privacy notice within legal terms, which could have the effect of putting-off readers, because of the length of the overall document.*

Privacy notices need to convey detailed information

GDPR Article 13(1) and (2) set out what information has to be included in a privacy notice where personal data is collected from the data subject.

WhatsApp noted the level of detail included in its privacy notice was consistent with the level of detail provided by its peers. The DPC dismissed this, noting that an industry could not be allowed to set its own level of compliance. At the same time, the DPC commented there was an abundance of text that communicated very little, warning against long but uninformative notices. WhatsApp's point is, however, well made: The standard set out in the decision goes significantly beyond that of most privacy notices. Indeed, a glance at the privacy notice on the website of the EDPB shows it does not meet the (very similar) standard applicable to the EDPB. Nor does the Irish DPC practice what it preaches. A substantial amount of work will be required to provide the level of transparency required.

Notice to non-users

The decision held that WhatsApp did not comply with its obligations under GDPR Article 14 (transparency obligations in relation to data obtained other than directly from the data subject). The decision acknowledged that the processing carried out by WhatsApp about non-users was very limited. It stated the main impact of the processing would be when a non-user signs up to WhatsApp (as this then reveals to other WhatsApp users the fact that this person is now a

WhatsApp user). Accordingly, most emphasis should be given to provision of information as this point.

The DPC specifically accepted that WhatsApp would not need to provide information individually to non-users and that it would be undesirable for WhatsApp to do this.

Approach to sanctions

WhatsApp must make required privacy notice changes within three months; large, international controllers will be held to high standards

The DPC was instructed by the EDPB to require WhatsApp to make required changes to its privacy notices within three months of the date of the order (reduced from the six months proposed by the DPC). WhatsApp argued that compliance would require considerable challenges. The EDPB opinion rejected this, noting WhatsApp was of a size and had sufficient means to be able to achieve this.

Similarly, the DPC rejected arguments by WhatsApp that the DPC should show similar leniency in its approach to smaller, national controllers; the DPC noted that large, international controllers with significant resources and in-house compliance teams will be held to a higher standard.

Quantum of fine

In setting the level of the fine, the DPC paid particular regard to:

- *the nature and gravity of the breach: Commissioner Helen Dixon noted that privacy information enables data subjects to exercise other rights and so is the "cornerstone of rights of data subjects" – accordingly she regarded this as a serious breach;*
- *the duration of the breach: considered to be ongoing since May 25, 2018; and*
- *the very large number of data subjects potentially affected.*

The Commissioner noted that relevant mitigating factors were the limited nature of data processed about non-users and the changes already made by WhatsApp to the privacy notices – however, she considered that no significant weight should be applied to these factors.

Overall, the Commissioner considered that a fine should be set at €225 million (being the sum of the separate fines proposed for breaches of GDPR Articles 12, 13, 14 and 5 respectively).

GDPR Article 83(4) and (5) provide for a cap on fines, set at the higher of a specified monetary or turnover-based amount. The EDPB opinion noted the relevant turnover is that of "all the component companies of the single undertaking," which would be the turnover of the group headed by Facebook Inc. The EDPB Article 65 decision directed the DPC to consider WhatsApp's turnover not solely when ensuring that the fine did not breach the cap, but also when setting the level of the fine initially.

The EDPB opinion also instructed the DPC to impose a higher fine for the infringements identified. In considering this, the DPC benchmarked its decision against the €50 million fine imposed by the CNIL against Google.

The DPC calculated the proposed fine by adding together separate fines proposed for breach of GDPR Articles 12, 13, 14 and 5. GDPR Article 83(3) provides that "if a controller or processor intentionally or negligently, for the same or linked processing operations, infringes several provisions of this Regulation, the total amount of the administrative fine shall not exceed the amount specified for the gravest infringement." In the original decision notice, the DPC referred to this provision and interpreted this as meaning that the fine would be limited to the highest of the separate fines proposed for breaches of the various articles of the GDPR. The EDPB opinion considered this interpretation to be incorrect; it stated that the provision should be interpreted instead as meaning that the total fine – for all the infringements – should not exceed the relevant fine cap as set out in Articles 83(4) or (5). Accordingly, the DPC recalculated the fine on this basis.[xx]

The lesson here is that organisations should never feel confident that they have provided sufficient information in their privacy notices. Data protection supervisory authorities may always use a complaint as an opportunity to demand greater transparency and to punish your organisation.

Purpose limitation

The purpose limitation principle requires your organisation to specify the purpose or purposes for its processing at the outset. Decent DPOs ensure that the purposes for gathering the personal data have been decided before the collection starts. Collecting 'nice to have' data is challenging (if not illegal). Your organisation can't use personal data for new purposes if the purposes are 'incompatible' with the original purposes for collecting the data. But, even if the new purpose is compatible with the original purposes, you must ensure that your organisation also has a legal basis it can rely on (for example, legitimate interest) for the new purpose.

This principle has become more challenging to observe as big data and Artificial Intelligence have become more and more advanced. One of the founding principles of these fields is to harvest vast amounts of data and try to find new ways of using it over time. With the speed of development, it is very hard to foresee new purposes even a year in advance, and practically impossible two or three years from now. Every organisation I've worked with has not been able to imagine future uses of the data it has and describe them in its current privacy notice, so don't worry too much if your organisation fails in this respect, either.

Some laws, including the GDPR, contain more detail on assessing compatibility with existing purposes. Instead of a general exemption for research purposes, the GDPR's purpose limitation principle specifically provides that it does not prevent further processing for archiving purposes in the public interest; scientific or historical research purposes; or for statistical purposes. Processing for other types of research purposes need very careful evaluation before they can be commenced with any confidence.

If it is determined that the new purpose doesn't fall within the scope of the research exemptions, your organisation will need to consider how the new purpose scan me made sufficiently transparent to affected individuals, and whether, in extremis, it is necessary to seek the affected individuals' consent before the new processing commenced. Be very wary of the consent route. If consent is required, what will your organisation do when individuals either refuse to consent or, at a later stage, withdraw the consent they had previously given? Decent DPOs will venture down the consent route only when all other options are unavailable.

Data minimisation

Theoretically, adhering to the principle of data minimisation is probably one of the easiest ways for your organisation to stay out of trouble. If your organisation hasn't got it, the information can't be compromised. Your organisation must ensure the personal data that is being processing is adequate (i.e. sufficient to properly fulfil the stated purposes; relevant (i.e. has a rational link to the purposes); and limited to what is necessary (i.e. don't not use any more information than is needed for the purposes).

In terms of deciding what is adequate, relevant and limited, decent DPOs will carry out case-by-case reviews.

To assess whether it is holding the right amount of personal data, your organisation must first be clear about why the data is needed. For special category data or criminal offence data, it is particularly important to make sure that your organisation collects and retains only the minimum amount of information. For example, to deliver goods, your organisation probably only needs the name and address of the customer. It doesn't need to know the customer's income or marital status. On the other hand, if the purpose is for credit assessment, the customer's address, income and marital status will probably be very relevant.

Your organisation should also periodically review the processing to check that the personal data that is held is still relevant and adequate for its purposes and that that anything longer needed has been deleted. Data that was considered necessary at one time may no longer be relevant now. Decent DPOs schedule annual reviews of the wording of registration or application forms and ensure that the information that is transferred from the forms to their organisation's information systems is changed when it becomes clear that the information being requested is no longer necessary. If, for example, an individual's birthdate is necessary because they can't receive a service until they reach a certain age, then once they have reached that age (e.g. 18) it won't be necessary to record anything about their birthdate other than the organisation has received evidence that they are older than a certain age. Taking another example, if individuals are required to show their COVID 19 passports to access a particular venue, it isn't necessary for that venue to record the dates on which the COVID vaccinations were dispensed to that individual.

Be careful when your organisation's marketing team announces that it wants to retain information in order that it can profile individuals. Customer profiles can quickly become out of date. Like fashions, personal tastes change. If it doesn't think there are sufficiently strong grounds for retaining it, your data protection supervisory authority is likely to dismiss the explanation that your organisation had decided to retain customer information because it had fairly disclosed this fact in its privacy notice and because it had sufficient storage space. The authority may even treat this matter as an aggravating factor when considering what enforcement action to take in the event of a personal data breach.

Accuracy

The importance of holding correct data cannot be exaggerated. Inaccurate or incorrect data can, when processed, result in very negative effects on individuals, such as wrongful decisions and mix-ups. All personal data must be accurate and, if necessary, kept up to date and it must not be misleading. Your organisation must carefully consider any challenges to the accuracy of personal data. In practice, this means that your organisation must take every reasonable step[xxi] to ensure the accuracy of any personal data; ensure that the source and status of personal data is clear; carefully consider any challenges to the accuracy of information; and consider whether it is necessary to periodically update the information. This is a high bar for most organisations to meet.

Your organisation must always be clear about what it intends the record of the personal data to show. What it is used for may affect whether it is still accurate or not. For example, just because personal data has changed doesn't mean that a historical record is inaccurate – but they must be clear that it is a historical record, rather than a current record.

One good way to maintain accurate and up-to-date information is to encourage individuals themselves to keep their details up to date via a user portal. Another way could be to ask for confirmation at every user interaction, or at certain intervals.

Your organisation could also, if necessary, consult external resources, such as public records of addresses and contact details, and check its data against these. This is a common practice in many business sectors – for example, debt collection – but you should make sure that your organisation's privacy notice explains what information is being checked, and with whom.

I've often advised call centre staff that is very important to make clear and contemporaneous notes of interactions with customers. Should callers be rude to staff, I've asked staff to record the actual words or phrases that the customer used. A note on the customer's file simply saying "customer was rude" isn't enough. Rudeness is a subjective term that can be defined in a variety of ways, so recording the facts, however disagreeable, is preferable to recording a staff member's impression of the customer's behaviour. With accurate records of the customer's behaviour, the customer can either be dealt with by appropriately trained staff, or ultimately denied a service should they persist with their bad behaviour. Decent DPOs remind their organisations that it has a duty of care to its staff. It is not fair to expect staff to put up with obnoxious and unruly people, especially when they complain in person or by phone. People may not like it if, when making a Subject Access Request, they realise that their bad behaviour has been recorded, but they have no right to demand that your organisation deletes the record just because they are now apparently embarrassed at their past behaviour.

It is especially important to ensure that accurate data is held by staff that are required to operate whistleblowing schemes. These schemes are increasingly common and are important ways of preventing and finding out about corruption and other forms of non-approved or illegal behaviour, such as sexual harassment. A key challenge with whistleblowing schemes is that in most cases the records contain free-text fields that anyone can use or abuse. The likelihood of mistakes or malpractice is therefore quite high. Information that is clearly of no interest or relevance to a case may be reported – for instance, a whistleblower might report a colleague for fraudulent activities and inadvertently include the names of family members of their colleague in the report. The personal data of the family members should not then be processed further within the case or investigation (unless it is relevant of course). Nor should any information revealing the identity of whistleblowers be disclosed to senior managers without good reason.

A much harder case to handle is the mischievous allegation, where an individual just wants to damage someone else's reputation. On the one hand, once the allegation has been made, the data relating to it is correct in the sense that it reflects what has been alleged; on the other hand, the content of the allegation itself is wrong (i.e. not accurate). Should the content be deleted from the whistleblowing record because the allegation was wrong, or should it be kept because the data accurately reflects what the whistle-blower stated in the allegation? Whether or not the data is deleted, how long it is kept and what aspects of the data are kept must be assessed on a case-by-case basis. Decent DPOs are likely to conclude, particularly after having conducted a Data Protection Impact Assessment on the whistleblowing process, that no data associated with an investigation should be erased, but that all irrelevant data should be redacted or otherwise prevented from being accessed by the investigation's decision makers. Maintaining these Chinese walls isn't easy – but it must be done.

Storage limitation

Your organisation must not keep personal data for longer than is needed. You need to think about – and be able to justify – how long it is kept. This will depend on the purposes for holding the data and the possible harm that may be caused to individuals should that data be compromised.

Your organisation needs a policy setting standard retention periods wherever possible, to comply with documentation requirements. You should also periodically review the data your organisation holds, and erase or anonymise it when no longer needed.

Your organisation must carefully consider any challenges to the retention of data. Individuals have a 'right to erasure' if the data is no longer needed – but in many regulated industries, organisations have an obligation to retain certain types of data, and this retention obligation overrides the individual's right to object.

Most organisations find this principle incredibly hard to observe, given the difficulty in deleting data that is so often so hard to locate, particularly when it is buried in electronic archives or in paper form in warehouses. As server space have become cheaper and cheaper, the necessity of continually erasing data to save space has diminished. In the past, many organisations had to delete data to keep their server costs down. That is no longer the case. Your organisation will most probably have collected vast amounts of data without ever thinking about the need to delete it. Decent DPOs need to be aware of the presence of any old data. Try asking your IT department if they have, or know of, any old legacy systems or databases and conduct a random sample check of the data in those systems. You are very likely to find some data that should have been deleted.

A key challenge for many organisations is that so much data is processed in interlinked databases for a variety of purposes. There are real fears that deleting some data fields might have catastrophic consequences for reports that are routinely generated, even though your IT teams may have not documented the details of all recipients of the reports. To help manage this, your information governance teams should maintain documentation to ensure that every data point in a system shows both its purpose and its retention period. Decent DPOs must have a good understanding of their organisation's business model and the purposes for which their organisation's data is processed in order to be able to monitor whether data is being kept for too long.

Even when the data can be easily found, data custodians face huge challenges in determining whether it will have any future value. Some data protection professionals consider that there are hidden benefits of retaining information that might otherwise be deleted. The historians of the future may be dismayed at the amount of information that is considered of no value today being destroyed if its retention would have adduced valuable insights into today's society. Electronic storage costs continue to fall, and your organisation should not use 'data protection' simply as an excuse to delete data indiscriminately.

Data protection supervisory authorities recommend that each time it collects data, your organisation should define what data is necessary, the purpose of the data collection and for how long the data should be kept, for example in a purpose and retention matrix. For this to work in practice, your organisation should assign data owners to each set of personal data. The data owners should be responsible for maintaining sets of Records of Processing Activities as well as ensuring that all requirements, including deletion, are met throughout the data lifecycle.

To enable good retention and archiving governance, your organisation should maintain a corporate policy and publish general schedules with specified retention periods. The schedules should include data categories, purposes, retention periods and the reasoning behind each retention period – for example, the legal requirement (and if so, the relevant law). The schedules should preferably be created as a matrix or table. Without them, your organisation will find it hard to know what to keep and what to delete. If possible, data should also be tagged (e.g. with metadata) with these periods in your systems right from the point of collection. It may also be necessary for specific departments to set up their own retention schedules.

Adding to this complexity, some of these purposes may be affected by a request to be forgotten. I've already explained that in most cases, legal requirements to retain data overrule deletion requests. When your organisation processes personal data on the legal basis of consent (e.g. for marketing), however, it must stop the processing when such a request is received.

The 'right to be forgotten' has turned out to be more of a vacuous soundbite, used by politicians to promote the merits of the GDPR as it was going through the European Parliamentary stages. It is not really a right that most people can exercise. Don't worry about deletion requests too much. You organisation ought to be capable of justify its data retention practices. With the notable exception of communications data, where there has been great interest in the private data that is mostly retained for law enforcement (which falls within the scope of EU competencies) and national security (which falls outside the scope of EU competencies) purposes, it's not a principle that many data protection supervisory authorities have spent much time enforcing.

Integrity & confidentiality

Organisations must process personal data securely by means of *appropriate technical and organisational measures*[xxii] – this is also known as the 'security principle'. Your organisation must carry out a risk analysis, develop policies, and take appropriate physical and technical measures to protect the data. You and your colleagues must also consider what is the state of the art and the costs of implementation when deciding what measures to take. The measures must be appropriate both to your organisation's circumstances and the risk the processing poses. This means that the same level of security is not needed for everything – it depends on what personal data is being held and the purpose of the processing.

Where appropriate, your organisation should look to use measures such as pseudonymisation and encryption to protect personal data. Other measures must be implemented to ensure the confidentiality, integrity and availability of business systems and services and the personal data processed within them. These measures must also enable your organisation to restore access and availability to personal data in a timely manner in the event of a physical or technical incident. Such measures also include training staff to ensure that they know what is expected of them. Remember, specific training needs to be provided to those that have specific responsibilities, such as the Subject Access Request team and the data custodians.

Data protection supervisory authorities also expect your organisation to ensure that appropriate processes are in place to test the effectiveness of these measures and undertake any required improvements. You'll have to maintain and a lot of paperwork to keep the authorities happy.

The difference between data protection & information security

How can you draw a clear distinction between the concept of data protection and information security? In Europe, according to the GDPR, data protection relates to *the protection of natural persons in relation to the processing of personal data.*[xxiii] This concept is linked to Article 8(1) of the Charter of Fundamental Rights of the European Union and Article 16(1) of the Treaty on the Functioning of the European Union, which provides individuals with the right to the protection of personal data concerning them.

Information security is only mentioned once in the GDPR. This is because the GDPR doesn't specify what an acceptable level of information security is. It merely sets requirements for organisations that use personal data to have adequate processes that ensure that their use is lawful, fair and transparent. Personal data must, however, be processed in a manner that ensures the appropriate security of personal data, including protection against unauthorised or unlawful processing and against accidental loss, destruction or damage, using appropriate technical or organisational measures.[xxiv] This refers to what within the information security world are called the principles of confidentiality, integrity and availability.

Decent DPOs need to know that the information security principles concern:

- confidentiality – access restrictions are in place and data is secured from unauthorised access;
- integrity – keeping data intact, unchanged and accurate over its whole lifecycle; and
- availability – information is available to authorised persons when they need it.

Data protection legislation consists of many more requirements and obligations. Data protection is therefore much wider in scope than information security, as it covers all aspects of the *use* of personal data.

In developing a good culture of privacy and data protection practice within your organisation, you should focus on good information governance matters and you should expect your information security lead to be accountable for developing and maintaining good information security practices. It is important though that you at least have a basic knowledge of decent IT security. You should ensure that this basic knowledge covers the topics of encryption, firewalls, access management, monitoring, back-up systems, passwords, authentication, information classifications and security awareness.

You won't need to be an expert in the field of data loss prevention ("DLP") – your information security lead should be accountable for this. As malicious intruders have become more proficient at what they do, and as the consequences of personal data breaches have become more severe, the need to monitor how data flows around your organisation has become increasingly important. DLP software monitors user behaviour and the data flows in an organisation. Typically, DLP solutions control the endpoint activities, reading and monitoring data streams on corporate networks. There are numerous ways in which DLP can be used in data protection management – for example, controlling whether data is sent to unauthorised cloud solutions or whether external emails can be sent with attachments in a specific format.

Your chief concern will be when the use of DLP solutions involves the monitoring of employees, as this constitutes an intrusion of the privacy of employees. From a data protection perspective, this is a dilemma. To what extent should the legitimate interest of your organisation (to protect its systems, fulfil its obligations under the GDPR, etc.) prevail over the interest of employees' privacy, and how transparent should your organisation be about how it monitors employees? The answer to this question will depend on the type of data your organisation is processing, and the extent to which any misuse might harm individuals or your organisation. The more transparent you can be, the better.

Many organisations also require their employees to only or mainly use business equipment and systems that are provided to them for work-related purposes. Employees should use their own equipment for sending and receiving their own personal communications, and they should do this in their own time and at their own expense. Your organisation has every right to use appropriate monitoring systems to ensure that this happens. If employees are told that that they may use corporate systems for limited personal use, they should be given no expectation that any such use is private. Increasingly, organisations are prohibiting employees from using corporate equipment for any personal purposes, as it is so hard to control work-related information on personal devices. Decent DPOs will agree with me that 'bring your own device' policies have caused consternation amongst information technology security teams. Group WhatsApp and Signal chats should likewise be discouraged.

Accountability

The GDPR's supporters have claimed that one of the changes brought about in Europe by the GDPR is the explicit introduction of the accountability principle.[xxv] However, this is not a new concept.

In 1980, the Organisation for Economic Cooperation and Development ("OECD") first published privacy guidelines that included an accountability principle. Little work was done to define accountability or to describe what it meant for organisations to be accountable for the responsible use and protection of data until September 2009, when the Centre for Information Policy Leadership published a paper entitled 'Data Protection Accountability: The Essential Elements", which set out the conditions organisations would have to meet to be accountable. [xxvi] The paper was the result of the Galway Accountability Project, an initiative facilitated by Ireland's Office of the Data Protection Commissioner and co-sponsored by the OECD. The Galway Project enlisted specialists from twelve countries, and the participation of privacy protection agencies from Europe, Asia and North America. Consumer advocates and business representatives also took part. As the project's secretariat, the Centre served as principal drafter of the paper, which considered the concept of accountability as it applied in an environment where data collection and use is ubiquitous, data flows are difficult or impossible to track, and jurisdictional issues abound as data crosses national borders. It was hoped that the paper would bring a critical international perspective to the dialogue on changing privacy law in Europe, the United States and Canada.

In November 2009, Peter Hustinx, the then European Data Protection Supervisor, announced that accountability would figure prominently in a joint initiative to develop global standards led by the Spanish Data Protection Agency. Later that month, during the 31st International Conference of Data Protection and Privacy

Commissioners held in in Madrid, a resolution was passed proposing that organisations should no longer only be responsible for being compliant, they must also be able to demonstrate that they are compliant, at any given point in time.[xxvii] This became known as the Madrid Resolution. However, it took over 7 years - until the coming into force of the GDPR - for the resolution to have any legal effect.

Accountability, as reflected in the UK GDPR, means that your organisation must document all parts of its data protection work (including Data Protection Impact Assessments, training records, incident logs, Records of Processing Activities, records retention schedules, current and former privacy notices, etc.) and adopt appropriate internal policies. This involves you monitoring a lot of work. Even in the absence of any known incidence of non-compliance, your organisation must be able to show what has done and what plans have been made to comply with legal requirements and regulatory expectations. As the DPO, it is your job to ensure that all relevant documentation is in place and up to date, just in case a data protection supervisory authority asks to inspect any of them. It's also your job to track progress on the deliverables that have been planned. This may well be a Sisyphean task, but it's why decent DPOs earn decent salaries.

I'll say more about the accountability principle in my letter on priorities.

3 TRANSLATING THE LAW INTO PRACTICAL STEPS

Data protection by design

Data protection by design is a phrase which appears in the GDPR[xxviii] and essentially describes the approach that your organisation should take to ensure that privacy and data protection issues are taken into account at the design phase of any system, service, product or process and then throughout the product or data lifecycle. This is not a new concept. When developing new systems, policies and processes, embarking on data sharing initiatives or when using data for new purposes, your organisation must:

- put in place appropriate technical and organisational measures designed to implement the data protection principles; and
- integrate safeguards into their processing so that they meet legal requirements and protect individual's rights.

A key focus for your organisation should be to ensure that robust information security measures are adopted and maintained to prevent a personal data breach. Data protection supervisory authorities will expect to see evidence that robust technical measures are being implemented in practice; that these measures are being documented and kept up to date; and that risk assessments are continuously being undertaken to identify critical systems and potential weaknesses which could pose a threat.

Fortunately, the Information Commissioner's Office has published guidance explaining the security standards it expects responsible organisations to have in place. The ICO's Enforcement Notices against British Airways[xxix] and the international hotel chain Marriott[xxx] in October 2020 include useful comments on the scope of the security measures that the ICO is likely to consider necessary.

In interpreting the requirement that appropriate technical and organisational security measures should be adopted, the ICO made extensive references to industry standards and technical guidance issued by various third parties when evaluating the failures that it found BA to have committed. It also took a broad approach to assessing the circumstances under which the requirement applies. The ICO rejected BA's argument that the obligation to take appropriate technical and organisational measures only applied to systems which process personal data. Your organisation needs to apply the same standard to all aspects of its network which could pose a threat and result in a personal data breach being committed.

The ICO also regarded several technical measures as being insufficient within BA. While the gaps identified in the enforcement notice are specific to the case, they still provide a useful insight into the regulator's expectations. The ICO was concerned about the employment of breach detection measures (e.g. logging and scanning for code changes); the active management of supply chain risks; and the need for multi-factor authentication for remote access to an internal network through an external device.

Measures highlighted in the Marriot enforcement notice included the appropriate monitoring (including logging) of privileged user accounts and database activity; while the measures Marriot took to safeguard against PCI DSS risks was insufficient. The ICO was also concerned that while payment card data is likely to be the highest risk category, other tables, depending on the sensitivity of the data held (such as passport numbers) also represent a significant risk to individuals when compromised and warrant some types of alerts. The ICO also noted that Marriot's decisions on what types of security measures were considered appropriate should be documented in risk assessments to demonstrate the evaluative judgement it arrived at.

Data protection by default

Data protection by default requires your organisation to ensure that only the personal data that is necessary to achieve a specific purpose is processed. This concept is linked to the key data protection principles of purpose limitation and data minimisation. I say more about this my letter on applying the privacy principles.

Data protection by default means that your organisation must specify what personal data will be used before the processing starts, appropriately inform individuals and only process the data needed for that purpose. It does **not** require you to adopt a 'default to off' solution. You just need to ensure your organisation has thought about the issue.

Your organisation must consider:

- adopting a 'privacy-first' approach with any default settings of systems and applications;
- ensuring individuals are not offered an illusory choice regarding the data that will be processed;

- not processing additional personal data unless the individual allows this;
- ensuring that personal data is not automatically made publicly available to others unless there is a good reason, such as the individual decides to make it so; and
- providing individuals with sufficient controls and options to exercise their rights.

In considering whether to take appropriate enforcement action against an organisation, a data protection supervisory authority will review the technical and organisational measures that organisations have put in place to address 'data protection by design and default' obligations. Instead of a fine, the ICO could issue an Enforcement Notice for any failings.[xxxi] Enforcement notices aren't any easier to manage than fines as they extend your organisation's engagement period with the ICO. With a fine, the direct engagement with the ICO ends as soon as the fine is paid, and the ICO offers a 20% discount to prompt payers. When an enforcement notice is published, which typically requires specific measures to be taken within a specific time period, the engagement will only end when the ICO is satisfied that the required actions have been taken. This extends the direct engagement with the ICO for, potentially, many months. I say more about the regulator's enforcement powers in my letter on regulators.

Data processors

If you use another organisation to process personal data on your organisation's behalf, then that organisation is a data processor. Before starting to use them, your organisation must be provided with sufficient guarantees to implement appropriate technical and organisational measures to meet the requirements of local data protection laws and ensure the protection of the rights of individuals.[xxxii] Don't think that your organisation can avoid regulatory censure because a personal breach occurred while personal data was being processed by that other organisation. If your organisation can't provide evidence to explain that the breach occurred in spite of the measures it took to supervise the processing, it is likely to face some sort of censure. Your organisation's reputation will always be at risk when another organisation does your work for you.

Decent DPOs are wary of falling into the trap of outsourcing too many functions, including customer care functions, to third parties. You may then fall victim to the third party's change control systems which effectively prevent your organisation from obtaining urgent changes to customer-facing processes.

Subject access requests

One of the stronger rights that individuals have is the right to understand how and why organisations are using their data, and to check it is being done lawfully. Individuals are entitled to:

- confirmation that their personal data is being processed;
- a copy of the information that compromises their personal data (not copies of the original documents that contain this information); and
- other supplementary information – this largely corresponds to the information that should be provided in a privacy notice. I've listed these categories in my letter on transparency.

As your organisation has a legal duty to respond to these requests, it's helpful to ensure that the applicant puts their request in writing as soon as possible – so that in the event of a subsequent dispute, the facts concerning who requested what and when are clear. Although there is no legal requirement for an individual to make their request in writing, your organisation should try to get the individual to acknowledge that they have made a request as soon as possible. There is also no legal requirement for an individual to make their request directly to the data protection team, so your organisation should ensure that all call centre staff are trained to understand when a request is made know how to refer the request to the team that will be responding to it.

It's helpful to ensure that before call centre staff refer a request to the data protection team, the applicant would either already have been authenticated or they would have been advised what extra steps will be taken by the data protection team to authenticate them. The key to this is proportionality. Your organisation cannot insist that particular types of identification (e.g. copies of driving licenses) be provided if an individual can be appropriately authenticated using other means.

Most organisations have produced Subject Access Request forms which enable individuals to include all the details that might be needed to locate the information they want. However, they cannot insist that individuals use these forms. Your data protection supervisory authority would be extremely unhappy if your organisation were to refuse to start to respond to a request until a specific application form had been completed and returned. In many cases, especially when application has been made electronically, your organisation can respond by sending emails and email attachments to the applicant,[xxxiii] but there may be times when an applicant insists that the information be provided to them in another form, perhaps in paper form. To reduce the costs and delays that are associated with dealing with these requests, the most efficient organisations enable applicants to serve themselves by accessing and downloading "their" information directly. This approach works best in cases where the individual had previously supplied the information themselves and now just wants to access it. The approach doesn't work as well when applicants seek to access notes that were written, say, by call centre staff, as there is a risk that these notes could have been poorly drafted and, if provided in their current state, present the organisation in a bad light. Your organisation has every right to ensure that what is provided to individuals is grammatically correct and doesn't contain spelling errors.

Although a Subject Access Request relates to the data held at the time the request was received, in many cases organisations will be routinely updating or deleting information that has reached its retention limit. Your organisations is therefore allowed to supply the information that is held when the response is despatched even though it may be slightly different to that which was held when the request was received. Unlike legal holds, your organisation is not required to retain data past its ordinary retention date just because the information may be needed to deal with a subject access request.

Your organisation must provide individuals with their personal data in an intelligible form using clear and plain language. If your organisation uses commonly uses acronyms to describe an individual or their circumstances, the meaning of these acronyms must be properly explained. If the information was originally recorded in a foreign language, though, your organisation is not required to translate it. Equally, handwritten information in a document that is illegible need not be deciphered.

When subject access fees were abolished in the UK in 2018, many organisations encountered a significant increase in the volume of such requests. Until 2018, the token £10 fee helped dissuade many individuals whose main purpose for making an application was to cause an unnecessary amount of work to be carried out by the organisation. Individuals often used their Subject Access rights to express their dissatisfaction about the way they have been treated. It was a way of wreaking their revenge. Now, your organisation can only charge a fee for complying with the request when an applicant requests further copies of their data following a request. The fee must be based on the administrative costs of providing further copies of the information and should not simply be used to dissuade applicants from making further requests.

Requests should be acted on without undo delay and at the latest within one calendar month of receipt. The deadline to respond can be extended by a further two months if the request it is complex. The individual must be told within one month of your organisation receiving the request that it will take longer than a month to deal with it, and they must receive an explanation as to why the extension is necessary.

Individuals can nominate a third party to act on their behalf to make Subject Access Requests. Sometimes, this will be a solicitor acting on behalf of their client. In all cases, your organisation needs to be satisfied that the third party making the request is entitled to act on behalf of the individual. It is the third party's responsibility to provide evidence of this entitlement. They may be able to provide your organisation with a written authority to make the specific request, or they may have a more general power of attorney.

Financial services organisations have received speculative Subject Access Requests from claims management companies that purport to act on behalf of the individual. These companies frequently make bulk requests, many of which may be speculative in nature, as the claims management company may not know which organisations their client has a relationship with. Despite what these companies may claim, there is nothing in law to stop organisations that receive bulk requests dealing directly with the individual concerned rather than their 'agent'. Recipient organisations may contact the applicant themselves to check that the claims management company does represent them and they may send the results of the request directly to the applicant. The individual may then choose whether to share the information that has been disclosed with the third party once they have had an opportunity to review it. When it is suspected that speculative requests are routinely being sent to organisations that have no relationship with their client, decent DPOs should ensure that the relevant trade bodies consolidate the complaints from their members and raise the matter with the data protection supervisory authority.

There will be cases where an individual does not have the mental capacity to manage their own affairs, and in these such cases your organisation is entitled to make a reasonable assumption as to who has the appropriate authority to engage with it.

Occasionally, children may make Subject Access Requests, or your organisation will receive requests from people with parental responsibility. If you are confident that the child is mature enough to understand their rights, your data protection team should usually respond to the child. Alternatively, the team can allow the parent to exercise the child's rights on behalf of their child if the child authorises this, or if it is evident that this is in the best interests of the child. Such requests need to be handled with extra care, as the team may not know whether the child's parents are engaged in a domestic dispute, and whether this information will actually be used for the purposes of the dispute between the parents, rather than to assure the child that the organisation is using their personal data appropriately.

In Scotland, a person aged 12 years or over is presumed to be of sufficient age and maturity to be able to exercise their right of access, unless the contrary is shown. This presumption does not apply in England and Wales or in Northern Ireland, where competence is assessed depending upon the level of understanding of the child.

The stage at which a child is capable of giving their consent for medical purposes in England and Wales was settled in 1985 following the decision in a court case where a mother (Mrs Gillick), a very religious woman, failed to prevent her daughter from obtaining birth control services from her doctor. Although the daughter was under the age of 18, and therefore in legal terms a minor, the House of Lords held she was sufficiently mature to appreciate the consequences of her request. "Gillick competence" is now a term used in medical law to decide whether a child can consent to their own medical treatment without the need for parental permission or knowledge. As summarised by child psychologist Tessa Davis:

- competence enables a child to explain their own reasons in their own words;
- if a child is under pressure, their consent won't be valid, even if they have capacity;
- competence can change if the decision is more complex or if the child is under a lot of stress; and
- the child's parents don't have to agree. It's better to get parental agreement, but it's not necessary.[xxxiv]

When considering borderline cases, the ICO expects your organisation to consider:

- the child's level of maturity and their ability to make decisions like this;
- the nature of the personal data;
- any court orders relating to parental access or responsibility that may apply;
- any duty of confidence owed to the child or young person;
- any consequences of allowing those with parental responsibility access to the child's or young person's information. This is particularly important if there have been allegations of abuse or ill treatment;
- any detriment to the child or young person if individuals with parental responsibility cannot access this information; and
- any views the child or young person has on whether their parents should have access to information about them.

Responding to a Subject Access Request may involve providing information that relates both to the individual making the request and to another individual. Your organisation does not have to comply with the request if it would mean disclosing information about another individual who can be identified from that information, unless:

- the other individual has consented to the disclosure; or
- it is reasonable to comply with the request without that individual's consent.

In determining whether it is reasonable to disclose the information, your organisation must consider all the relevant circumstances, including:

- the type of information that would need to be disclosed;
- any duty of confidentiality owed to the other individual;
- any steps taken to seek consent from the other individual;
- whether the other individual can give consent; and
- any express refusal of consent by the other individual.

The decision will involve balancing the data subject's right of access against the other individual's rights. If the other person consents to the organisation disclosing the information about them, then it would be unreasonable not to do so. However, if there is no such consent, your organisation must decide whether to disclose the information anyway.

Your organisation cannot refuse to provide access to personal data about an individual simply because they obtained that data from a third party. It can, however, refuse to comply with a Subject Access Request if it is manifestly unfounded or excessive. The available options are:

- to request a "reasonable fee" to deal with the request; or

- refuse to deal with the request.

If your organisation refuses to comply with a request, it must inform the individual about:

- the reasons the organisation is not taking action;
- their right to make a complaint to the ICO or another supervisory authority; and
- their ability to seek to enforce this right through a judicial remedy.

In September 2019 the Government announced proposals to help organisations that were struggling with SARs. It acknowledged that many organisations, especially SMEs, lacked the capacity to process requests, particularly when they were received in bulk, and that occasionally the requests were being used for questionable purposes, or *in ways whereby the processing of personal data does not appear to be the sole or primary reason for exercising the right of access.* As the consultation paper described the problem:

There is a risk that Subject Access Requests may be used as a means of circumventing strict disclosure (of information and inspection of documents) protocols that would otherwise need to be followed under the Civil Procedural Rules in the context of actual or prospective litigation. As set out in guidance by the ICO, the general position under current law is that a controller cannot consider the purpose of a subject access request unless it seems apparent that the request is 'manifestly unfounded', whereby the data subject has no intention of exercising their right of access, or where the subject access request is 'malicious in intent' and is 'being used to harass an organisation with no real purpose other than to cause disruption'. The government is aware that some organisations believe that the threshold of 'manifestly unfounded' makes it difficult for data controllers either to navigate instances in which it would be appropriate to enquire about the purpose of the request, or to provide sufficient grounds for a refusal to comply with a request.[xxxv]

To address these issues, the government invited comments on a proposal to introduce a fee regime similar to that in the Freedom of Information Act 2000, which provided for access to personal data held by all data controllers, not just public bodies. The fee regime would be structured so as not to undermine an individual's right to access their personal data – although it's not clear what this restriction would actually mean in practice.

The existing FOI regulations[xxxvi] set a cost limit as £600 for central government and £450 for public bodies outside central government, such as local authorities. This regime gave public bodies the option of either refusing to deal with the request or charging a fee for responding. The consultation paper explained that a fee charging regime was already in place for public bodies for subject access requests relating to unstructured manual data. If a similar fee regime were introduced for all subject access requests, organisations (both public and non-public) would still be obliged to deal with the request to the extent possible within the cost limit - for example, by suggesting to the individual the information they may be able to search for, retrieve or extract within the cost limit. The cost limit would not function as a ground on which to refuse outright to deal with a request.

Decent DPOs will look forward to the outcome to this consultation exercise.

Right to object to marketing

The strongest data protection right is arguably the individuals' right to object to the processing of their personal data for direct marketing purposes.[xxxvii] This is an absolute right and there are no exemptions or grounds for organisations to refuse. On receipt of an objection to processing for direct marketing, your organisation must stop processing the individual's data for this purpose.

However, this does not automatically mean that the individual's personal data must be erased, as in many cases it will be preferable to suppress their details. Suppression involves retaining just enough information about them to ensure that their preference not to receive direct marketing is respected in future.

Right to object to other forms of processing

Individuals have qualified rights to object to the processing of their personal data in a range of situations.[xxxviii] Whether it applies depends on your organisation's purposes for processing and what lawful basis it relies on for the processing. These rights are not easy for many organisations, let alone individuals, to understand, and I don't expect that there will be many occasions when individuals will try to exercise them. You should seek specialist help when this issue arises. In brief, your organisation must inform individuals of their right to object at the latest at the time of the first communication with them where:

- personal data is processed for direct marketing purposes, or
- the lawful basis for the processing is because it is carried out in the public interest or as a public task, or for the organisation's legitimate interests.

Some individuals may object to the processing of personal data when your organisation uses legitimate interest as the legal basis for the processing. In these circumstances your organisation can continue processing the personal data if:

- it can demonstrate compelling legitimate grounds for the processing, which override the interests, rights and freedoms of the individual; or

- the processing is for the establishment, exercise or defence of legal claims.

When your organisation decides it has compelling legitimate grounds which override the interests of an individual, it should consider the reasons why the individual has objected to the processing of their personal data. If an individual objects because the processing is causing them substantial damage or distress (e.g. the processing is causing them financial loss), the grounds for their objection will have more weight. Your organisation needs to balance the individual's concerns with its own interests and must be able to demonstrate that its legitimate grounds override those of the individual.

When your organisation is satisfied that it does not need to stop processing the personal data in question, the individual should be notified. The decision should be explained, and the individual should be informed of their right to make a complaint to the ICO or another supervisory authority; and their ability to seek to enforce their rights through a judicial remedy.

When your organisation processes personal data for scientific or historical research, or statistical purposes, the right to object is more restricted. Nor do individuals have a right to object if the lawful basis for processing is because it is necessary for the performance of a task that is carried out in the public interest.xxxix

Should your organisation more than occasionally receive objections about the processing, it should review its fair obtaining notice to ensure that individuals are clearly notified about the processing. The more transparent your organisation is, the less it is likely that individuals will want to object to the processing. But your organisation must stop processing the data if it has received an objection and there are no grounds to refuse it.

The law does not specify how individuals should make a valid objection. They can be made verbally or in writing. Objections can also be made to any part of your organisation, there does not have to be to a specific person or contact point. So, make sure that all staff have been trained on how objections should be identified and managed.

Well run organisations have a policy for recording details of the objections they receive, including whether they were made by email, telephone or in person. The policy will usually require staff to check with the individual that they have understood their request, as this can help avoid later disputes about how the objection has been interpreted. If your organisation has such a policy, you should regularly review the logs to ensure that the procedures are working well. Your organisation must act on the objection without undue delay and at the latest within one calendar month of receipt. For practical purposes, if a consistent number of days is required (e.g. for operational or system purposes), it may be helpful to adopt a 28-day period to ensure compliance is always within a calendar month.

Your organisation can extend the time to respond to an objection by a further two months if the request is complex or if several requests have been received from the individual. Make sure you let the individual know within one month of receiving their objection and explain why the extension is necessary.

Right to be forgotten

Individuals have the right to have their personal data erased. This is also known as the 'right to be forgotten'. The right is not absolute and only applies in certain circumstances:

- if the personal data is no longer necessary for the purpose which organisations originally collected it for;

- if your organisation is relying on consent as the lawful basis for holding the data, and the individual withdraws their consent;
- when your organisation is relying on legitimate interests as the basis for processing and there is no overriding legitimate interest to continue this processing;
- when individuals object to the processing of their personal data for direct marketing purposes;
- when your organisation has processed the personal data unlawfully (i.e. in breach of the lawfulness requirement of the transparency principle); or
- when your organisation has processed the personal data to offer information society services to a child.

If a valid erasure request is received and no exemption applies then your organisation will have to take steps to ensure erasure from backup systems as well as live systems. Those steps will depend on an organisation's circumstances, retention schedules (particularly in the context of its backups), and the technical mechanisms that are available at the time.

Your organisation must be clear with individuals as to what will happen to their data when their erasure request is fulfilled, including in respect of backup systems. It may be that the erasure request can be instantly fulfilled in respect of live systems, but that the data will remain within the backup environment for a certain period until it is overwritten.

The key issue is to put the backup data 'beyond use', even if it cannot be immediately overwritten. Your organisation must ensure that the data is not used within the backup for any other purpose, i.e. that the backup is simply held on its systems until it is replaced in line with an established schedule. Provided this is the case, it is unlikely that the retention of personal data within the backup would pose a significant risk.

The right to be forgotten is not an absolute right. It does not apply if the processing is necessary:

- to exercise the right of freedom of expression and information;
- to comply with a legal obligation;
- for the performance of a task carried out in the public interest or in the exercise of official authority;
- for archiving purposes in the public interest, scientific research historical research or statistical purposes where erasure is likely to render impossible or seriously impair the achievement of that processing;
- for the establishment, exercise or defence of legal claims;
- for public health purposes in the public interest (e.g. protecting against serious cross-border threats to health, or ensuring high standards of quality and safety of health care and of medicinal products or medical devices); or
- for the purposes of preventative or occupational medicine (e.g. where the processing is necessary for the working capacity of an employee; for medical diagnosis; for the provision of health or social care; or for the management of health or social care systems or services). This exemption only applies where the data is being processed by or under the responsibility of a professional subject to a legal obligation of professional secrecy (e.g. a health professional).

Data collected from children

Children have the same rights as adults over their personal data. These include the rights to access their personal data; request rectification; object to processing and to have their personal data erased. An individual's right to erasure is particularly relevant if they gave their consent to processing when they were a child.

The ICO's Age-Appropriate Code, formerly known as the Children's Code, came into force in September 2021 and set out strict requirements for any organisation that provided "information society services" to children.[xl] This included all organisations that provide services, apps, games and web and social media services where children are likely to have access.

The Code adopted the UN Convention on the Right of the Child definition, which defines a child as anyone under the age of 18. I've already explained in this letter that the stage at which a child can give their consent for medical purposes in England and Wales was settled in 1985 following the decision in a court case where a mother (Mrs Gillick) failed to prevent her daughter from obtaining birth control services from her doctor. For the benefit of doubt, the Data Protection Act 2018 provides that children can give their valid consent if they have reached the age of 13.

The Code requires organisations to adopt the following standards:

- best interests of the child – ensuring that children and their safety is at the heart of consideration, and a primary concern when identifying what data needs to be collected;
- use of data protection impact assessments – this is a mitigation tool, used to identify risks and record the actions carried out to address those risks;
- age-appropriate application – child ages will vary, and therefore there will be children at different stages of their development. This needs to be considered when designing the privacy settings imposed by your organisation. This could be a blanket standard for all of those under 18, or a more tailored approach;

- transparency – organisations must provide information in a format that a child can understand;
- detrimental use of data – in essence, do not use children's data where it may be detrimental to their wellbeing;
- policies and community standards – organisations must document what they set out to do in their internal policies, and review and update where necessary;
- default settings – this is where the privacy settings should automatically be high with regards to the collection of children's data. For example, not collecting any more data than absolutely necessary to carry out your organisation's service or function;
- data minimisation – this is where your organisation collects the minimum amount of data necessary;
- data sharing – not to share the data unless it is in the best interests of the child;
- geolocation – any location tracking should be turned off by default;
- parental controls – if parental controls are in place, ensure the child is aware and understands how their data is being monitored by their parents;
- profiling – any form of automated processing should be automatically switched off. It should only be used if it is in the best interest of the child;
- nudge techniques – do not use nudge techniques to encourage children to provide any personal data. A nudge technique is a prompt or positive reinforcement technique used to encourage users to provide certain details, or follow a certain route;
- connected toys and devices – ensuring any toy organisations provide also conforms to the code; and
- online tools – providing support to children in order to enable them to exercise their rights. If your organisation process data collected from children, it should respect

requests for erasure if the processing of the data is based upon consent given by a child. This is still the case when the data subject is no longer a child because a child may not have been fully aware of the risks involved in the processing at the time of consent.

Decent DPOs should note that the Code has considerable extra-territorial effect and has spurred the largest tech companies in the world to alter their business models. Journalist Chris Stokel-Walker explained:

The Age Appropriate Design Code looked like a limp bit of legislation when it was laid before parliament in June 2020. It was a code of practice developed by the UK's Information Commissioner's Office (ICO) – itself not known as the most powerful enforcer of rights – because it was required by the 2018 Data Protection Act. In all, 15 headline standards of age appropriate design were drawn up, and companies were required to follow them "to ensure their services appropriately safeguard children's personal data and process children's personal data fairly."

The code requires privacy settings to be high by default for children, to collect and retain only the minimum amount of data on users, and to have geolocation switched off and an opt-in option. Nudge techniques to encourage children to counter any of these settings are banned, while parental controls need to be implemented in a way that a child can understand.

At the time it didn't merit much coverage, and companies were given a grace period of around a year to implement its requirements. "This has very much gone under the radar," says Andy Burrows, the head of child safety online policy at the NSPCC, a children's charity. But now that time is upon us, with the code launching on 2 September, its real impact can be seen.

That impact is unexpected, even to those with a hand in helping bring it into existence. "One of the things that's quite amusing about the Age Appropriate Design Code is that it was a compromise," says Ben Greenstone, founder of Taso Advisory, and an advisor to the government between 2014 and 2019, who worked under successive digital ministers near the end of his tenure in government. Baroness Kidron, chair of 5Rights Foundation, a child-focused charity, refused to support the UK's Data Protection Bill – later to become the Data Protection Act – as it passed through parliament. The government needed her support to pass the bill, so they offered her a sop.

"Government does this more than I think it'd like to admit," says Greenstone, "where it accidentally conceives of a policy as a way to allow something to pass." It was a classic case in government, he explains: people weren't fully across the entire field, and had a tough bill to get through parliament. So they tacked on a relatively simple amendment requiring the ICO to develop a code for approval. "It doesn't get everyone thinking: 'Oh god, this is going to be terrible.' But once it's reasonably foreseeable, if you're not compliant with the Age Appropriate Design Code, you're probably not compliant with the GDPR. And if you're not compliant with the GDPR, you'll have a metric shit ton of fines. So you have to do it."

And tech companies have done it – not that they'll publicly admit the code is the reason. A slew of changes by major technology companies in the last few weeks, from Tik ToK's control over direct messaging for those under the age of 18 to Google's offer of a right to be forgotten for teenagers who find images uploaded by parents or guardians in search results, to Instagram's change on August 30 to ask users their age, have all been designed to adhere to the incoming code in the UK, which has since been renamed the Children's Code. "All of them are announcing important safety protections," says Burrows. "And all of them are curiously omitting the principal reason for them – the fact that this regulation is coming in."

None of the platforms have explicitly mentioned the imminent code in their announcements of new features – by design. "They're saying: 'We're doing this because we think it's important'," says Greenstone. "You get a PR win in every country that isn't the UK, and you comply to the UK." Burrows thinks that the lack of acknowledgment of the code when announcing the new features and policy changes is due to fear. "The UK is putting down a marker here about how to regulate and how to take some bold steps to protect children from the range of online harms." If Big Tech makes an explicit public link between their changes and the code, it emboldens other legislators to take similar strident action – chopping down the power of Big Tech.

Greenstone is less certain whether major technology platforms are cowering, however. "I don't think it's a chink in Big Tech's armour," he says. "It's a slightly annoying administrative cost, but [they'll think]: 'It makes it significantly harder for anyone to compete with us.'"

Nonetheless, each of the changes made by the major tech platforms has an underlying principle, says Burrows: trying to engineer a culture change in the companies where children and their rights are seen as an important constituent group of users – not just in terms of the commercial return organisations can get from them, but also in protecting them. "This is a really important step," he says. "It's a step along the journey. But it's not the end destination."

However, it's clear that the changes have come about because of pressure from the UK to adapt to the new rules – and that's shocked those who thought the UK was a relative minnow in might when it came to bringing tech firms to heel. "It's proved more possible to make meaningful change than many companies like to think," says Sonia Livingstone, professor of social psychology at the London School of Economics, who studies children's rights in the digital age. Livingstone believes the arrival of the Children's Code has highlighted two things that weren't anticipated when it first came into existence. "One, to protect children you had to make changes to the entire internet, and two, that data protection has become a means of managing personal safety," she says. "In both those regards, people have been a bit taken aback, but that's just the nature of the internet now."

The platforms have followed the letter of the law because they know that doing so is important in the UK. However, that doesn't explain why they haven't simply integrated the required changes in the UK only, and kept their products and services the same elsewhere. "I think they can see the writing on the wall," says Livingstone. The UK's movements are part of a broader shift by governments globally to try and crack down on the power of major technology companies and tame them, and the platforms recognise that. "If you look at all the debate around online companies and how ethical or otherwise they are around data about children, if you're already making the changes in the UK, you should just do it globally because it doesn't change your service," says Greenstone.

Of course, the challenge is whether any missteps under the code are actually adjudicated on by the ICO – something Burrows and Greenstone are both waiting to see. "It said it's going to tackle where it sees the greatest sources of harm, and there'll be keen eyes here in the UK and in California to see how quickly off the mark the ICO acts," says Burrows. Greenstone points to the fact that the ICO has said it's going to take a gently-gently approach, indicating that the lack of concrete action speaks volumes about the ability of the ICO's 800-strong workforce to come up with meaningful legislation.

Nonetheless, Big Tech's new moral compass around children is welcomed – and whether they choose to admit it or not, Britain's Children's Code, designed to appease an obdurate peer to vote for a piece of legislation struggling to make it through parliament, has changed the way platforms approach underage users.

Livingstone has been surprised with the way her peers in the world of child rights have been swept up and hired by major technology companies. "They hire us, and then those folk assure us it's in their business interest that they want to do the right thing," she says. "We want to help families and be supportive of society. We have your values at heart.' That has become their PR style. What they have invested in it, I don't know. Maybe they do really fear the power of governments."[xli]

Right to port information from one organisation to another

The right to data portability gives individuals the right to receive personal data they have provided to an organisation in a structured, commonly used and machine-readable format. It also gives them the right to request that your organisation transmits this data directly to another organisation. It only applies when:

- The lawful basis for processing this information is consent **or** for the performance of a contract; and
- the processing is being carried out by automated means (i.e. excluding paper files).

Information is only within the scope of the right to data portability if it is the personal data of the individual they have directly provided to the organisation. This may include:

- history of website usage or search activities;
- traffic and location data; or
- 'raw' data processed by connected objects such as smart meters and wearable devices.

Derived data (e.g. information that is created from the dissemination and analysis of data, also known as profiled data) is out of scope. If this derived data is personal data, your organisation still needs to provide it to an individual if they make a subject access request. In practice, few people are likely to request that their data be ported to another organisation. How it ever became a fundamental right is beyond me. You should try to ensure that your organisation delivers the right by either:

- directly and securely transmitting the requested data to the individual; or
- providing access to an automated tool that allows the individual to extract the requested data themselves.

Individuals can also ask for their personal data to be transmitted directly to another organisation. If it is technically feasible, your organisation should do this. When considering what is technically feasible, remember that the right does not oblige your organisation to create transmission systems which are technically compatible with those of other organisations.[xlii] But, your organisation should not put in place any legal, technical or financial obstacles which slow down or prevent the transmission of the personal data to the individual, or to another organisation. Data must be transmitted in a structured, commonly used and machine-readable format.[xliii] The formats may include the comma-separated value (CSV) format, the Extensible Markup Language (XML) format or in the JSON open file format. In most cases, your organisation cannot charge a fee to comply with a request for data portability.

However, there may be legitimate reasons why the transmission cannot be undertaken. These reasons may include the cost of the transmission system and the low anticipated uptake. It is your organisation's responsibility to justify why these reasons are legitimate and why they are not a 'hindrance' to the transmission.

When your organisation provides information directly to an individual or to another organisation in response to a data portability request, it is not responsible for any subsequent processing carried out by the individual or the other organisation. However, it is responsible for the secure transmission of the data and need to take appropriate measures to ensure that it is transmitted to the right destination.

If your organisation accepts and retains ported data, it becomes your responsibility to ensure that all the legal requirements are complied with. As a recipient, your organisation needs to ensure that it has an appropriate lawful basis for processing any data. If it has received personal data which it has no reason to keep, it must be deleted it as soon as possible.

In practice, few people are likely to request that their data be ported to another organisation. How it ever became a fundamental right is beyond me. The data protection trainer Tim Turner commented: "*I remember a conversation with someone from a big consulting firm pre GDPR. The text was not fixed and so while we knew the shape of it, we didn't know the detail. "Portability" he said "is going to be a chuffing game changer". He didn't say chuffing.*

This is not to say he was wrong because if portability had ended up the way we understood it was going to be, I think it could have had a transformative effect. As it is, portability was heavily neutered and has limited application.

For reasons only they can explain, ICO illustrates portability as an imp carrying away the head of someone it has very cleanly decapitated. In fact, it's best understood as a heavily qualified subset of subject access.

You can get a copy of accessible, machine-readable personal data, but only if you provided it to the organisation or if it was obtained by monitoring your use of a service or a device. Moreover, this only applies if the data was obtained with consent or under a contract.

Any data generated by the controller (except via monitoring) or someone else is therefore not covered. Data obtained under a legal obligation or power isn't covered. The sound you just heard is the public sector switching off, as this barely touches most of their work.

I remember EU types talking about leaving a service and taking your data with you, but even the transfer provisions apply only where "technically feasible" which doesn't sound like an obligation to change internal systems to facilitate data exchange.

Private sector companies – especially those involved in fitness or other monitoring – clearly need to have processes in place to deliver machine readable datasets on demand. There may be business benefits to standardising how data is structured to make transmission easier.

This isn't the advertised tip or a hint: it's more a question. Who is portability in its current form *for*? What problem does it solve? Every other right has an obvious (if sometimes very specific) application. Is there any point putting measures in place for portability?[xliv]

According to data protection consultant Emma Butler: *I always thought portability was a daft thing to bring in. It was always clearly a consumer rights issue, not a data protection issue, especially as the access right gives you everything (unless exemptions apply, yes I know).*

As far as I remember, the banking industry was already looking at delivering on porting data through open banking and I think energy providers have to do more these days on providing info on your usage to help you compare and switch providers. Mobile phone providers also provide usage info as a matter of course. I don't think adding it into data protection law is particularly useful or helpful. But then, as we all know, the GDPR was drafted to get Facebook and Google and the Commission was under the illusion that a great EU alternative would come along and wanted people to be able to easily switch over. So now all organisations must manage a right that isn't very useful, and no-one exercises.[xlv]

So, don't worry too much if your organisation hasn't developed any data porting tools. You can leave that task to your successor.

4 ACCEPTING RISKS

As the DPO, you are not personally liable for data protection compliance: it is your organisation's responsibility to comply with data protection legislation. Nevertheless, you clearly play a crucial role in helping your organisation meet its data protection obligations.

Try not to feel paralysed into indecision by the enormity of what you do and the moral conundrums. Be firm and decisive but, at the same time, let your conscience and moral compass be alive and kicking.

I mentioned in my letter on doing the right thing that psychologist Oliver Burkeman considers that *the future will never provide the reassurance you seek from it.*[xlvi] The spiritual teacher Jiddu Krishnamurti said his secret was simple: "I don't mind what happens." Try not to live each day anxiously braced to see if things work out as you hoped.

The risk assessment process

With the risk assessment process, organisations take a good look at themselves to:

- identify processes and situations that may cause harm, particularly to people;

- determine how likely it is that each hazard will occur and how severe the consequences would be; and
- decide what steps can be taken to stop these hazards from occurring or to control the risk.

It's important to note the difference between hazards and risks. A hazard is anything that can cause harm, such as a failure of internal procedures or information security controls. A risk, on the other hand, is the likelihood, high or low, that a hazard will actually cause an individual any harm. As part of the risk assessment process, your organisation should identify the hazards and then assess the risk that individuals will be harmed.

Risk assessments are carried out by responsible organisations for a variety of reasons, including:

- providing an analysis of possible threats;
- preventing injuries;
- meeting legal requirements;
- creating awareness about hazards and risk;
- creating an accurate inventory of available assets;
- justifying the costs of managing risks;
- determining the budget to remediate risks; and
- understanding the likely return on investment.

Risks are often documented on a chart with two primary dimensions: probability and impact, each represented on one axis of the chart. This allows the risk management team to determine priorities and allocate resources to remediate the risks. Often, risk charts are colour coded, with high probability / high impact red risks featuring in the top right quadrant, and low probability / low impact green risks in the bottom left quadrant. Depending on the complexity of your organisation's risk assessment process, the charts may feature 4, 9, 16 or 25 sectors.

Organisations don't have to use charts – although they are easier on the eye and are more likely to attract the attention of a busy senior management team than the more basic spreadsheet approach. There's nothing wrong with the spreadsheet approach – even the ICO uses them. The ICO's risk assessment for COVID 19 risks in its offices took the for of a simple spreadsheet[xlvii] comprising seven columns documenting, with respect to each identified risk:

- What are the hazards
- Who might be harmed, and how?
- What are you already doing to control the risks?
- What further action do you need to take to control the risks?
- Who needs to carry out the action?
- When is the action needed by?
- Date complete

Data protection impact assessments

Data protection risks are documented by carrying out Data Protection Impact Assessments ("DPIA"). They are mostly conducted on new projects rather than existing processes. The purpose of the assessment is to analyse the intended or existing processing of personal data and help identify and minimise data protection risks systematically and comprehensively. A DPIA does not have to eradicate all the risks, but it should help your organisation minimise the risks and assess whether any remaining risks are acceptable.

DPIAs are required for processing that is likely to be 'high risk', but you shouldn't expect only to conduct assessments on initiatives whenever there is a likelihood that individuals will be exposed to some type of harm. Decent DPOs will ask for a DPIA to be conducted just to ensure that the project team has systematically considered the data protection implications of the initiative, and that other teams within your organisation have been appropriately engaged. A DIPA will also ensure that the executive accountable for the initiative is aware of any data protection issues and is prepared to be accountable to your senior management team if a data protection supervisory authority were to investigate and take enforcement action because your organisation failed to sufficiently respect the data protection principles. You don't need to be personally accountable for accepting risks – you just need to ensure that there is someone who will be accountable.

The earlier in the life of the project that the assessment is conducted, the greater is the likelihood that any significant risks will be identified and mitigated at little cost and with minimal disruption. This is why it is important to embed DPIAs into your organisation's project processes. When an early milestone in the project process is that the project team has evidenced appropriate engagement with the privacy team, you are more likely to be engaged in good time. A DPIA is not always a one-off exercise. You should see it as an ongoing process when assessing major projects, and regularly review the assessment to ensure that, as the project evolves, it does not result in the emergence of new and unanticipated privacy risks. I find it helpful to ask the project team for a progress update every 6 or 9 months on key projects – it lets them know that I'm keen to keep working with them and that I'll be checking up to ensure that any privacy-related tasks they had agreed to undertake are in hand.

The first question your organisation will usually ask you is whether it is necessary to conduct an assessment on a particular project. The ICO considers[xlviii] that an assessment must be conducted if the answers to any of the following trigger questions result in a positive response:

- Will the project involve the collection of new information about individuals?

- Will the project compel individuals to provide information about themselves?
- Will information about individuals be disclosed to organisations or people who have not previously had routine access to the information?
- Will the organisation use information about individuals for a purpose it is not currently used for, or in a way it is not currently used?
- Does the project involve the organisation using new technology which might be perceived as being privacy intrusive? For example, the use of biometrics or facial recognition.
- Will the project result in the organisation making decisions or acting against individuals in ways which can have a significant impact on them?
- Is the information about individuals of a kind particularly likely to raise privacy concerns or expectations? For example, health records, criminal records or other information that people would consider to be particularly private.
- Will the project involve the organisation contacting individuals in ways which they may find intrusive?

The European Data Protection Board considers[xlix] that the following types of processing require a DPIA as they are likely to fall within the 'high risk' threshold:

Innovative technology & Artificial Intelligence

Artificial Intelligence (AI) is an umbrella term for a range of algorithm-based technologies that solve complex tasks by carrying out functions that previously required human thinking. Decisions made using AI are either fully automated, or with a 'human in the loop'. As with any other form of decision-making, individuals impacted by a decision supported by an AI system should be able to hold someone in your organisation accountable for it.[l]

Experts such as Professor Michael Jordan, a leading researcher in AI and machine learning at the University of California in Berkley, have commented that AI systems are nowhere near advanced enough to replace humans in many tasks involving reasoning, real-world knowledge and social interaction. AI systems show human-level competence in low-level pattern recognition skills, but at the cognitive level they merely imitate human intelligence and don't engaging deeply and creatively.

According to Professor Jordan, when the term was coined in the 1950s, people aspired to build computing machines that possessed human-level intelligence. That aspiration still exists, but computers have not become intelligent per se. Instead, they have provided capabilities that augment human intelligence. Despite such developments being referred to as 'AI technology,' the underlying systems do not involve high-level reasoning or thought: *AI technologies do not yet form the kinds of semantic representations and inferences that humans are capable of. They do not formulate and pursue long-term goals.*[li]

Professor Ian Brown of the Oxford Internet Institute agrees with this analysis. They are not as advanced as people would perhaps like them to be: *as far as AI means anything, it is systems with some element of learning from data.*[lii]

Artificial Intelligence technologies are very hard for privacy professionals to assess because, usually, very few people understand the logic that the algorithms use, and it can often be extremely difficult to persuade third party suppliers to share enough information about the algorithms and the weighting that is used in their AI systems to provide sufficient assurance that it is not biased in any meaningful way, nor does it rely on irrelevant or excessive data. You should still go through the DPIA process, though, and try to ensure that the assessment does document what is known about how automatic decisions will be taken. Even the fact that so few people in your organisation have any idea as to how the 'black box' works is an important fact to document. You are likely to conduct an assessment if the project concerns:

- connected and autonomous vehicles;
- intelligent transport systems; or
- smart technologies (including wearables).

Denial of service

Your organisation may want to take decisions about an individual's access to a product, service, opportunity or benefit which are based to any extent on automated decision-making (including profiling) or involves the processing of special category data. You are likely to conduct an assessment if the project involves:

- credit checks;
- mortgage or insurance applications; or
- other pre-check processes related to contracts (e.g. for mobile phones).

Large-scale profiling

Your organisation is expected to take several factors into account when determining whether the profiling is sufficiently *large scale* to trigger the obligation to conduct a DPIA. These factors are:

- the numbers of data subjects concerned;
- the volume of personal data being processed;
- the range of different data items being processed;
- the geographical extent of the activity; and
- the duration or permanence of the processing activity.

Despite criticism from data protection professionals that list was too vague, the EDPB decided not to agree on a single metric, which is a shame as it makes the decision on whether to conduct an assessment more complicated. The Estonian Data Protection Inspectorate has been much more helpful and has suggested[liii] that data processing is of large scale when it concerns:

- special categories of personal data or personal data relating to criminal offences of 5000+ people;
- personal data of high risk of 10 000+ people; or
- other personal data of 50 000+ people.

I use a simpler test: which is whether the monitoring is likely to involve at least 10,000 people. However, I've never refused to conduct a DPIA simply because this threshold wasn't met. You are therefore likely to conduct an assessment if the project concerns:

- personal data processed by Smart Meters or IoT applications;
- hardware/software offering fitness/lifestyle monitoring services; or
- social-media networks.

Biometric data

A biometric is any measurable physical characteristic or personal trait that can be used to identify or verify an individual's identity. Biometric processing is becoming increasingly common, even though many data protection supervisory authorities are concerned about the way it can be used (and possibly abused) by organisations that don't adequately notify individuals of their practices. You are likely to conduct an assessment if a project concerns:

- facial recognition systems;
- workplace access systems/identity verification;
- access control / identity verification for hardware / applications (including voice, fingerprint and facial recognition); or
- CCTV systems which monitor individuals in public spaces.

Genetic data

Outside the health sector, very few organisations will process genetic data. However, you are likely to conduct an assessment if a project concerns:

- medical diagnosis;
- DNA testing; or
- medical research.

Data matching

Many organisations will at some stage want to combine, compare or match personal data that has been obtained from multiple sources. You are likely to conduct an assessment if a project concerns:

- fraud prevention;
- direct marketing; or
- monitoring the personal use or uptake of statutory services or benefits.

Invisible processing

Data protection supervisory authorities are concerned at the amount of processing of personal data that organisations carry out in circumstances where the data has not been obtained directly from the individual and where the provision of a fair obtaining notice would prove impossible or involve disproportionate effort. You are likely to conduct an assessment if a project concerns:

- list brokering;
- online tracking by third parties;
- online advertising;
- data aggregation or data aggregation platforms; or
- the re-use of publicly available data.

Tracking

Organisations quite frequently track an individual's geolocation or their behaviour, either in the on-line or off-line environment. Accordingly, you are likely to conduct an assessment if a project concerns:

- social networks, software applications;
- fitness, lifestyle or health monitoring;
- IoT devices, applications and platforms;
- online advertising;
- web and cross-device tracking;
- data processing at the workplace;
- data processing in the context of home and remote working;
- processing the location data of employees; or
- loyalty schemes.

Targeting of children and other vulnerable individuals for marketing, profiling for auto decision making or the offer of online services

Data protection supervisory authorities get very concerned when organisations use the personal data of children or other vulnerable individuals for marketing purposes, profiling or other automated decision-making. The assessment must ensure that, where appropriate, the provisions of the ICO's Children's Code[liv] effective from September 2021, have been adopted. I've said more about data collected from children in my letter on translating the law into practical steps. You are likely to conduct an assessment if a project concerns:

- connected toys; or
- social networks.

Risk of physical harm

Very occasionally, your organisation will be involved in a project where a personal data breach could jeopardise the physical health or safety of individuals. You are therefore likely to conduct an assessment if a project concerns:

- Whistleblowing / complaint procedures; or
- Social care records.

Data protection risks and privacy harms

A decent assessment should focus on whether the project in hand breaches data protection legislation, so the purpose of the exercise is to ensure that your organisation has sufficient evidence to demonstrate that the project complies with the key data protection principles that are themselves set out in your organisation's privacy policy. Linking the assessment to the privacy principles helps the privacy team embed these principles throughout the organisation:

Lawfulness, Fairness & Transparency

Personal data must only be handled where it is reasonable and lawful to do so. Your organisation must provide clear information to individuals about how it handles their personal data and for what specified business purposes.

So, how can your organisation justify the purpose of the processing and what legal basis would it rely on? Does the current Fair Processing Notice adequately explain what will happen to an individual's personal data, or will it need to be amended? If it does need to be amended, who will amend it, and by when? Or will a new notice need to be prepared just for those individuals who will be impacted by the new processing? If one does need to be prepared, who will amend it, by when, and what arrangements will be made to ensure that the impacted individuals can access it?

Purpose limitation

Personal data must only be handled for a specified business purpose and must not be used or disclosed in a way incompatible with that purpose. So, would an individual be surprised if they were to realise that their personal data was being processed for this purpose? How can your organisation justify the new purpose and what legal basis would it rely on?

Data minimisation

Only the minimum personal data that is required for a specific business purpose must be handled. So, what categories of personal data are going to be used? if new categories of personal data are going to be collected, who will be accountable should a data protection supervisory authority decide that an inappropriately wide range of information is being processed?

Accuracy & Relevance

Personal data must be accurate and relevant for the specified business purpose for which it is handled. If it is assumed (but you should check) that personal data within your organisation's existing systems will be monitored for accuracy in line with the standards set out in your organisation's Information Security Policy, what controls govern the personal data supplied by a third party? What controls will be put in place to ensure that personal data supplied or processed by a third party will be and remain accurate?

Storage Limitation

Personal data must be retained and disposed of in accordance with your organisation's Information Retention & Management Policy. So, who will ensure that any new personal data will be deleted in accordance with your organisation's data retention schedule?

Integrity and Confidentiality

Your organisation's Information Security Policy must be followed to ensure that personal data is protected from unauthorised or unlawful disclosure, transfer, loss, alteration or destruction. Who will ensure that any new personal data will be subjected to the same information security controls that prevent all your organisation's personal data from being corrupted?

A decent impact assessment should also review the following risks:

Choice, Access & Correction

Individuals' marketing choices must be respected, and they must have the ability to access and correct their personal data. If the proposed initiative relates to marketing, have adequate marketing permissions been built in to ensure that individuals who object to the use of their data for marketing purposes can be honoured? Also, will any new categories of personal data be held in business systems that enable an individual to easily access them should a Subject Access Request be made? Will these business systems also enable individuals to easily exercise their right to correct any inaccurate personal data?

Data Transfers

Appropriate controls must be imposed on suppliers and other 3rd parties that handle personal data on your organisation's behalf. Where personal data is transferred across borders, including within the organisation, such transfers must comply with relevant laws and regulations. So, who will ensure that the procurement and legal team has properly documented the transfers and that the correct contractual terms protect the personal data? I'll say more about this in my letter on international privacy issues.

Decent DPOs find it easy to structure an assessment that is based on reviewing compliance with these issues, as the document will refer to concepts that many people in your organisation should already be familiar with. If individuals are going to suffer any form of data protection harm, it is more than likely that it will be because insufficient care has been taken to ensure that one or more of these issues has been appropriately considered.

The DPIA should consider whether a failure to design safeguards to avoid compromising these issues would result in a risk that an individual would suffer a significant privacy harm. Many people struggle to understand the concept of significant privacy harms, but it is important that a DPIA sets out in plain language what the potential adverse impact on an individual would be. Professors Danielle Keats Citron of the University of Virginia School of Law and Daniel Solove of George Washington University Law School have created the following taxonomy to describe privacy harms:[lv]

- physical harms;
- reputation harms;
- emotional harms;
- thwarted expectation harms;
- economic harms;
- relationship harms;

- chilling effect harms;
- disturbance harms;
- informed choice harms;
- autonomy harms;
- data quality harms;
- vulnerability harms;
- control harms; and
- discrimination harms.

Although the ICO has published[lvi] a sample DPIA methodology, there is no reason why decent DPOs should not develop their own assessment template. The Article 29 Working Party has also recommended[lvii] a methodology for conducting assessments, but remember these are recommendations, not strict requirements that will automatically result in enforcement action if any element is absent in your organisation's assessment.

You'll only need to consult a data protection supervisory authority if your assessment identifies a high privacy risk and it is not possible to take any appropriate measures to reduce that risk. When this happens, your organisation won't be able to begin the processing until the authority has been consulted. Fortunately, there will, in practice, be very few times when your organisation should find it necessary to take this step. The closest I've ever come to referring an issue to the ICO has involved cases where accountable executives were initially not happy to be personally accountable for a privacy risk that related to one of their projects. Threatening to engage the senior management team if, say, the accountable executive refuses to accept any of the recommendations that you make on the DPIA may well result in the executive changing their mind!

Data protection audits & healthchecks

Data protection audits & healthchecks are usually carried out when your organisation needs a more holistic view of its data protection controls. One of the most effective business cases you can make to conduct an audit is to explain to your organisation that, in the event of it experiencing a personal data breach that must be notified to a data protection supervisory authority, the fact that certain controls have failed will become known to the authority. This will result in an increased risk that the authority will take a greater interest in the organisation. Should personal data breaches continue to be reported, the authority may decide to carry out a wider review of your organisation's data protection controls. As some authorities, including the ICO, have explained in some detail what controls should to be in place and operating effectively, your organisation ought to know how it will respond to the questions that every decent Data Protection Officer knows will be asked.

The ICO has published an accountability framework to help organisations evidence compliance with the key data protection controls.[lviii] The July 2021 version of the framework had 338 controls, and these controls will continually evolve as data protection accountability practices change over time. Don't be put off by the ICO's accountability tracker which, with 6 columns to use to input information about each control, suggests you will need to record and track progress regarding 2028 data points. You won't be solely responsible for tracking all of them. The ICO's framework prompts your organisation to shape job roles to ensure that data protection compliance is the responsibility of all staff at all levels.

The framework is particularly useful as it enables your organisation to conduct audits and healthchecks in 10 separate scope areas:

- leadership and oversight;
- policies and procedures;
- training and awareness;
- individuals' rights;
- transparency;
- records of processing and lawful basis of processing;
- contracts and data sharing;
- risks and data protection impact assessments;
- records management and security; and
- breach response and monitoring.

This accountability framework is an excellent way of framing your organisation's response when asked to explain how good it is at data protection. Your organisation may currently be grotty at data protection in quite a few of these scope areas, but the supervisory authorities are likely to look reasonably kindly on organisations that know how grotty they are and have plans, and can demonstrate progress on these plans, to improve their level of compliance. No organisation is perfect at this stuff. Every organisation I know is on a journey to compliance. Some organisations are a lot further ahead in their compliance journey than others.

All the large professional services firms offer data protection audits and healthchecks, and most test controls that are similar to those the ICO advocates. So, is it worth going for the methodology used by one of these firms, or is it better to adopt the ICO's approach? How do you choose between them? The main difference is that your organisation can use the ICO's methodology to generate pie charts and reports free of charge. The work can also be carried out in the timescales determined by your in-house staff. On the other hand, it is likely to cost your organisation a not inconsiderable amount to use one of the frameworks developed by a professional services firm – but in return for the fee that will be charged, they will probably carry out the fieldwork themselves. If your organisation lacks the staff to carry out the fieldwork but has the budget to subcontract the work to a professional services firm, you might as well go ahead with the firm's offering. The final report is unlikely to reveal anything you don't already know about the state of your organisation's compliance with regulatory expectations, but it may prove to be useful background material when you seek additional help (and resources) from the senior management team to carry out the remedial measures that will be highlighted.

Decent DPOs will need a good reason to explain to senior management teams why it would be appropriate to deviate from the ICO's approach. If I were you, I would use the free resources that the ICO has made so widely available.

I'll say more about this in my letter on priorities.

5 PRIORITIES

In my letter on doing the right thing, I mentioned psychologist Oliver Burkeman's comment that *there will always be too much to do – and this realisation is liberating*. There's no reason to assume that there will be any fit between the demands on your time – all the things you would like to do or feel you ought to do – and the amount of time available. The demands will keep increasing, while your capacities will remain largely fixed. It follows that the attempt to "get on top of everything" is doomed. Indeed, it's worse than that – the more tasks you get done, the more you'll generate.

The good news is that you needn't berate yourself for failing to do it all, since doing it all is impossible. The only viable solution is to make a shift: from a life spent trying not to neglect anything, to one spent proactively and consciously choosing what to neglect, in favour of what matters most. Former Information Commissioner Richard Thomas was always ready to remind those who criticised his office for inaction that his team had to be selective to be effective. Future historians will judge whether the correct calls were made during his time in charge.

Governance

You must avoid working for too long for an organisation that has an undocumented or ad hoc governance structure for its privacy and data protection issues. This way, disaster looms. One of the first and most important compliance actions you will need to complete following your appointment as DPO is to ensure that your organisation has an effective data protection governance structure in place. It is not enough for you to be appointed and expected to answer questions and address issues as they arise. You need to understand what your role is, and what data protection responsibilities are given to your co-workers. Before you can get much stuff done, it is vital that everyone understands who is responsible for doing what. You can then help your organisation move to the next stage of the good governance model, which is to ensure that all staff are doing whatever it is that they are responsible for doing.

I've worked with organisations where heads of departments were allowed to act independently and where there was little or no senior management oversight of issues pertaining to data protection risks and conflicting objectives. Tensions would occasionally flare up between the marketing team and the data protection team. A 'them and us' culture prevailed. A decent DPO will gain the senior management team's support to form a working group of a few key members of staff who have the mandate to make decisions and accept risks. Need you lose any sleep if the head of the marketing team is determined to do something that you are uneasy about? Isn't it a more productive use of your time to document the potential risks involved if the marketing campaign were to go ahead and ensure that the risk has been formally accepted by the accountable executive (i.e. the head of marketing)? Most marketing managers I've worked with did not want to accept personal responsibility for the consequences of any regulatory enforcement action regarding a marketing campaign I was uneasy about. Get the accountable executive to accept accountability for the risk in writing and you'll probably find that the marketing teams will soon change their plans.

With an efficient governance structure supporting you, you should have more time to act proactively. However, you'll always find yourself dealing with requests to comment on projects that have vague objectives and short deadlines.

Accountability: focus on your data protection programme

I mentioned in my letter on applying the privacy principles that one of the key changes brought about by the EU's General Data Protection Regulation was the explicit introduction of the accountability principle.[lix] This means that your organisation must document all parts of its data protection work (including Data Protection Impact Assessments, training records, incident logs, Records of Processing Activities, records retention schedules, current and former privacy notices, etc.) and adopt appropriate internal policies. This involves you curating a lot of paperwork. Even in the absence of any known incidence of non-compliance, your organisation must be able to show what has done and what plans have been made to comply with legal requirements and regulatory expectations. Decent DPOs will endeavour to ensure that all relevant documentation is in place and up to date, just in case a data protection supervisory authority asks to inspect it. Decent DPOs will also track progress on the deliverables that have been planned. Accountability brings with it a greater focus on the need to produce evidence to demonstrate compliance.[lx]

Accountability can be divided into three key stages:

- documenting the measures your organisation has in place to fulfil the applicable requirements and obligations. For example, have a governance document in place indicating how the senior management team has delegated data protection responsibilities within your organisation;

- recording the reviews your organisation carries out to show that these measures are in place; and

- documenting the information which demonstrates that the implemented measures are working effectively (i.e. that they have had the anticipated effect).

In terms of how you get accountability done, as a priority you'll need to ensure that your organisation has an internal data protection policy, i.e. a statement that sets out how your organisation protects personal data. It should contain a set of principles, rules and guidelines that informs how your organisation will ensure ongoing compliance with data protection laws. The ICO's data protection policy[lxi] is a good model to copy. At only 8 pages in length, it demonstrates that such policies don't have to be long documents.

Your senior management team ought to be familiar with the concept of an accountability framework, as it is a concept that is commonly used in other compliance areas (e.g. anti-corruption, anti-money laundering, export controls etc,). The frameworks are useful flexible and scalable tools. They help DPOs set out a vision for their organisation of what "good" looks like. They frame the data protection compliance journey, pointing to the evidence that regulators require for your organisation to demonstrate what progress has been achieved. You should think of data protection compliance as a journey that all organisations must embark on. You may have left your organisation well before it reaches its destination, but that's not your problem. Your senior management team needs to know not only what progress has been made, but also what else is likely to expected of it.

Choosing the right accountability programme

A wide range of methodologies have been developed to help organisations document their compliance obligations and evidence the extent to which they are meeting these obligations. A lot of work has been devoted to explaining what "good" looks like. The trick lies in selecting the right tool. Some tools have dashboards that present key information about the organisation's current risk profile and offer users the ability to generate automated reports on outstanding data protection tasks. Many of the compliance tools that are commercially available aim to ensure that all data protection-related documentation is available within one repository, potentially making it harder for an organisation to change providers when it becomes evident that they are using a suboptimal tool. You will probably want to avoid the trap of relying on a commercial tool until its potency has been proven and you are confident that your organisation can afford the subscription fees for the foreseeable future.

The Centre for Information Policy Leadership has devised an accountability framework[lxii] which focusses on seven key scope areas:

- Leadership and Oversight
- Transparency
- Risk Assessment
- Training and Awareness
- Policies and Procedures
- Monitoring & Verification
- Response and Enforcement

These scope areas have been further divided into the following issues:

- **Leadership and Oversight**
  tone from the top
  executive oversight
  data privacy officer/office of oversight and reporting
  data privacy governance
  privacy engineers
  internal/external ethics committees

- **Transparency**
  privacy policies and notices to individuals
  innovative transparency – dashboards, integrated in
  products/apps, articulate value exchange and benefits, part
  of customer relationship
  information portals
  Notification of data breaches

- **Risk Assessment**
  at programme level
  at product or service level
  data protection impact assessments for high-risk
  processing
  risk register
  risks to organisations
  risks to individuals
  records of processing activities

- **Training and Awareness**
  mandatory corporate training
  ad hoc and functional training
  awareness raising campaigns and communication strategy

- **Policies and Procedures**
  internal privacy rules based on data protection principles

information security
legal basis and fair processing
vendor/processor management
procedures for response to individual rights
others (e.g. marketing rules, HR rules, mergers &
acquisition due diligence)
data transfers mechanisms
privacy by design
templates and tools for data protection impact assessments
crisis management and incident response

- **Monitoring & Verification**
  documentation and evidence - consent, legitimate interest
  and other legal bases, notices, impact assessments,
  processing agreements,
  breach response compliance monitoring and testing -
  verification,
  self-assessments and audits
  privacy seals and certifications

- **Response and Enforcement**
  individual requests and complaints handling, breach
  reporting, response & rectification procedures
  managing breach notifications to individuals and regulators
  individual requests and complaints-handling & breach
  reporting, response and rectification procedures
  implementing response plans to address audit reports
  internal enforcement of non-compliance subject to local
  laws & engagement/co-operation with data protection
  supervisory authorities

In contrast, the ICO's accountability framework[lxiii] focusses on 10
key scope areas:

- Leadership & Oversight

- Policies & Procedures
- Training & Awareness
- Individuals' Rights
- Transparency
- Records of Processing Activities and lawful basis
- Contracts & data sharing
- Risks & DPIAs
- Records management & security
- Breach response and monitoring

I like the ICO's approach. The ICO has set out its expectations about what it would expect to be in place with regard to each scope area, together with indicators to help your organisation understand the types of measures that are likely to indicate that the ICO's expectations are being met effectively. These expectations have been influenced by its audits, investigations and casework. ICO initiatives such as these remove the uncertainty that many DPOs have had about what "good" looks like. Whether your organisation likes it or not, this is how the ICO will determine the extent of your organisation's data protection compliance. You should use the ICO's checklists and templates in presentations to your senior management team when explaining the data protection compliance journey that your organisation is on. The ICO's templates evidence not just what the ICO wants to see but how the ICO wants to see it. Within the 10 scope areas you'll find some 73 expectations and 339 measures that should be in place to meet the ICO's expectations.

For example, regarding management structures that provide leadership and oversight, the ICO expects that:

- there is an effective and clearly defined management framework providing oversight of data protection and information governance;
- your organisation has considered whether it needs a DPO under Article 37 and if it does, the role satisfies the

requirements and responsibilities outlined in the GDPR; and

- operational roles and responsibilities have been assigned to support data protection and information governance.

In terms of the types of measures that your organisation should have in place to meet the ICO's expectations effectively:

- there is an organisation chart showing the reporting lines and flow of information between any relevant committees and groups;
- the DPO is tasked with monitoring compliance with the GDPR and other data protection laws, data protection policies, awareness-raising, training and audits and
- there are operational roles in place and responsibilities are assigned to ensure the effective management of all records e.g. in job descriptions.

This is a lot of work for any organisation to be expected to evidence, but DPOs attending an accountability workshop with the ICO, facilitated by the Centre for Information Policy Leadership in October 2019, agreed that that the greater focus on evidence to demonstrate compliance was welcome.[lxiv]

If you're working in a global organisation, the ICO's accountability framework is also a very useful way of demonstrating to local data protection supervisory authorities that, regardless of the specific requirements of local laws and regulations, a global approach is being taken to addressing privacy obligations. It is evidence of a broader commitment to meeting international standards. Reports that indicate a good level of compliance with the ICO's framework ought to result in a certain degree of regulatory forbearance in the event of non-compliance with a local data protection requirement. Organisations need to be incentivised to adopt accountability programmes: the incentives should exist in the form of approved templates and industry specific examples of good practice. This is what the ICO's framework seeks to achieve.

Be careful when you prepare your initial compliance report though. Too heavy a focus on what is wrong with your organisation in terms of its failure to meet the ICO's expectations will result in you running a risk of being perceived as an encumbrance. Don't worry. Although it may look like it, you have not been appointed as the DPO purely to burden on your organisation with reams of unnecessary compliance stuff. The fact that your organisation's data protection compliance journey is likely to be long (or extremely long) may not be well received by your senior management team. But you have not been appointed DPO just to be a popular person. You are paid to be competent. Don't use the toolkit as a check list with a simplistic pass/fail outcome. Don't view your organisation through a single lens – of how much red there is on the chart. Not all the ICO's expectations are as important as others.

You'll probably be challenged to justify that your privacy programme is effective. What you're doing, you will argue, is simply being proactive. You'll be using the standard questions you know the ICO will ask of your organisation should it need to report a personal data breach, and in doing so you'll be forewarning your senior management team of the state of its compliance with the standards the ICO will expect to see embedded in a well-run organisation. Most well-run organisations will want to know what risks are being taken, in order that these risks can be formally accepted. Surely, it is better to know just how good or how grotty your organisation is, using an authoritative benchmark such as the ICO's accountability framework, rather than not knowing how it meets the ICO's expectations until it's too late.

This is your priority. You need to see (and document) the big picture, and you should try to spend at least half your time on it. No-one else is likely to be so narrowly focussed on the accountability programme, and everyone will expect you to drive the improvements that will be required.

Focussing on operational data protection issues should be your second priority. Your organisation will probably already have a team dealing with information rights requests (even though they may not directly report to you) and perhaps others will be conducting data protection impact assessments. They'll be asking you how to deal with the tricky issues that they face each day. Your legal colleagues will be working with their procurement colleagues to ensure that vendor contracts contain the correct data protection clauses. They'll also be asking you how to deal with the tricky issues that they face each day. They won't be the only ones though - you'll also need to block out sufficient time in your diary to deal with ad hoc requests from others in your organisation, as well as time to liaise with data protection colleagues outside your organisation. Keeping up to date with data protection developments is a constant challenge – so network amongst your colleagues and use the relationship your organisation has with its trade body to understand what lobbying work is being undertaken on your behalf.

6 REGULATORS AND THE LAW

Regulators are public servants who are expected to act independently. They are expected to apply the law of the land. They are not expected to interpret it as they would have liked the law to have been drafted but are instead required to offer practical guidance on aspects of the law to ensure that organisations such as yours take an appropriate approach to implementing the law in particular cases. European data protection supervisory authorities are also expected to coordinate their activities and agree on a common approach to enforcing privacy laws.[lxv]

But what the law requires is not always what the regulators deliver. The EU's data protection supervisory authorities don't always see eye to eye, and their decision-making capability has been greatly hampered the consistency mechanism - an over cumbersome consultation process created by the General Data Protection Regulation. It has enabled the more privacy-minded data protection supervisory authorities to prolong discussions within the European Data Protection Board on what enforcement action to take in particular cases to such an extent that the levels of trust and co-operation between the lead supervisory authority and other concerned supervisory authorities has frequently been in serious danger of breaking down.

Many members of the European data protection community breathed a sigh of relief on learning that Johannes Caspar was stepping down in June 2021 as head of the Hamburg Data Protection Commission after 12 years. Caspar had earned a reputation as one of Europe's less pragmatic and business-friendly regulators. Commenting on the GDPR just before his departure, he claimed that the Regulation suffered from massive flaws and had provoked endless infighting within the European Data Protection Board. As journalist Stephanie Bodonni reported in June 2021:

Tensions over GDPR have been welling up from the start. Overnight, the Irish Data Protection Commission was transformed into the leading EU supervisor for the Silicon Valley giants with regional hubs in the nation, such as Apple Inc. and Facebook Inc. With 28 Irish probes into tech firms pending and no immediate decision in sight, the authority has faced a barrage of criticism accusing it of being too slow and too soft.

"The basic model of the procedure set up by GDPR has massive flaws and it just can't work," Caspar said. "You can't accept this in the long term. The problem is what use are these laws to the people if they're not being applied?"

The 59-year-old German, who returns to academia after June 28, has earned a reputation as one of the EU's toughest regulators. He first made his mark in 2010 with his criticism of Google's Street View rollout and more recently he slapped a local Hennes & Mauritz AB unit with a 35.3 million euro ($42 million) penalty for snooping on staff, a probe that was opened and shut in less than a year.

One of the faults in the GDPR system, he points out, is the way it gives regulators "lots of room for interpretation" of the rules. "At the end of the day, our energies are spent on infighting."

A key feature of the law is the so-called one-stop-shop system that puts the authority in the country where a company has its EU base in charge of them. But this, too, has led to tensions. A dispute between Facebook and the Belgian watchdog over their powers to enforce an order against the social media giant ended up in the EU's top court, which ruled this month that other watchdogs can still weigh in on some cases.

Another complication is that probes into possible violations with an EU-wide effect can't be concluded by the lead authority alone. Colleagues from across the bloc need to sign off on decisions.

Helen Dixon, Ireland's data protection commissioner, was trapped in this process when she wanted to finalize her first Big Tech probe, concerning Twitter Inc. She has called criticisms over delays by her agency "ludicrous."

"The idea that 30 data protection authorities decide on cases through consensus and cooperation" means "we get lost in side issues," Caspar said.

Last month, he imposed a three-month banning order on Facebook to stop it collecting German users' data from its WhatsApp unit.

"This is an important case for the future of EU data protection supervision," Caspar said. The EU body of data protection regulators "could -- and this is what we're asking -- extend the measures beyond the three months and impose the same measures across Europe."

Leaving too much control in the hands of the lead authorities, such as deciding on when to open a probe and what the scope of the investigation should be without much room for input from others, creates tensions, he said.

"For me this is why such a system can't work," he said. "Authorities have to work fast and effectively to be able to give clearly deterring signs that certain behaviours are not OK. If that doesn't happen, law and reality are at odds.[lxvi]

In the UK, the ICO has enjoyed a mixed reputation. Its staffing levels have increased significantly over the past few years which, together with personnel changes at the most senior level, have resulted in the recruitment of a large cohort of staff that were new to the privacy field. It takes time for any privacy professional to establish themselves, and those working for the ICO found it equally challenging to meet the expectations that were placed upon them by those that rely on the ICO for support – both organisations and individuals who had complaints or concerns with organisations.

During my time with a financial services trade body in the 1990s, I was fortunately able to develop a close working relationship with key senior ICO staff. We would regularly attend the same data protection receptions, seminars and conferences, where much alcohol and canapés freely circulated at the end of the event. The trade body worked closely with ICO officials and industry representatives to produce data protection codes of practice on the (new at the time) Data Protection Act 1998. I helped draft the code that was developed for members of the Association of British Insurers[lxvii] and later a separate code for other members of other financial services trade bodies.[lxviii] As an employee of a trade body, my role was twofold: to explain key aspects of data protection law to member companies, and to describe the practical difficulties that member companies were encountering with the law to the ICO in the hope that it would help members adopt pragmatic solutions to knotty problems. This was a time when the ICO's focus was more on educating organisations about the law than taking enforcement action against those that flouted the law. Enforcement action would generally be taken only in the most egregious cases. The ICO's enforcement approach favoured the carrot rather than the stick.

My relationship with the ICO evolved as I worked for data controllers over the next 20 years. People I would have called friends at the ICO became colleagues. The working relationship with those at the ICO became more business-like and could get strained at times. As an employee of (and representing) an organisation, for example, there would be times when we did not share the same view on issues. When reporting data protection breaches, for example, it became more important for me to act at arm's length from those who worked in Wilmslow.

There were also times, however, when the company I was working for would liaise very closely with the ICO following a personal data breach. In one notable case, arguably the then Information Commissioner himself broke the law by inadvertently publicly revealing the identity of an organisation (mine) he was investigating following a data breach. Rather than commence legal proceedings against the ICO for breaching the Data Protection Act, my employer's investigators supported the ICO's enforcement team as they prosecuted an employee and a former employee for their unlawful acts. Despite their guilty pleas at the Crown Court, the miscreants weren't fined because they wouldn't have been able to afford to pay any fine. For the first time, the ICO worked with the Assets Recovery Agency to recover money that had been unlawfully obtained. Anything that had not already been transferred to their wives was at risk of being confiscated. The ICO's investigation team found working with the ARA to be a useful strategy. ICO fines are not kept by the Commissioner but are paid into the Consolidated Fund, the Government's general bank account at the Bank of England. On the other hand, the Commissioner is allowed to retain a small percentage of the money that is recovered under proceeds of crime litigation. It's not a significant sum, but it is more than enough to pay for a celebration dinner for the ICO's investigators at the best curry house in Wilmslow.

In that particular case, the ICO had quickly reached the view that the company I was working for was just as much of a victim of crime as were its customers. Also, the ICO had erred in identifying the company too soon. Accordingly, I was not placing it in any jeopardy by working extremely closely with the ICO's investigation team. Had that breach have occurred today, the ICO's investigators may well have taken a different view. Today, they may well have held the organisation liable for its failure to put in place sufficient information security controls to prevent the miscreants from using specific techniques to obtain and misuse the relevant personal data.

Some organisations may be tempted to argue, following a data breach, that they could not be held responsible for the activity of organised criminals who were involved in the attack. Today, the ICO is likely to disagree, emphasising that the reason for taking enforcement action will not be because a personal data breach occurred *per se*, but due to the failures of the organisation to take appropriate technical and organisational security measures to protect the personal data of its customers in the first instance.

Decent DPOs should appreciate that while investigating and responding to a breach and taking immediate steps to mitigate the damage caused are important, this may not be sufficient to prevent sanctions from being imposed on your organisation. Preventative measures are the key to avoiding enforcement sanctions.

Organisations are increasingly challenging the ICO's enforcement team and have recently had some notable success in reducing regulatory fines. In October 2020 the ICO announced a dramatic reduction in its fine against British Airways following a personal data breach. It had announced in July 2019 that it intended to impose a fine of £184 million for exposing the personal data of nearly 430,000 customers, but the penalty was later reduced to £20 million. After the ICO issued its notice of intent in 2019, British Airways challenged the basis on which the authority had calculated the fine that it sought to impose. Amongst its arguments was that the use of an unpublished draft internal procedure by the ICO to provide a guide on quantum, which referred to the turnover of the controller, was unlawful. This resulted in the ICO changing the way in which it calculated the fine and is thought to be one of the primary reasons for why the amount was reduced.

Data protection lawyer Dan Whitehead has explained that how BA responded to the incident was also relevant in lowering the fine:

While the sanction was imposed due to security failures that existed before the incident, the steps the airline took in its response resulted in the fine being reduced by £6 million (a 20% discount). These steps included the prompt notification of data subjects, regulators and law enforcement, BA's full cooperation with the ICO during the investigation, the offer to reimburse customers who suffered financial losses and the remediations that have since been taken to improve security. This reinforces the importance of organisations who suffer a data breach taking immediate action in responding to the incident, being co-operative with regulators and taking proactive steps to mitigate the damage caused to affected data subjects.

In practical terms and given the specific notification obligations set out in the GDPR, knowing how to react in the immediate aftermath of a data security incident is key. As more and more jurisdictions around the world introduce mandatory data breach notifications, making the right call in terms of who, when and how to notify is likely to have a direct effect on the enforcement approach adopted by regulators.

It is also important to note the mitigations which the ICO did not consider to be relevant in considering quantum. It dismissed the significance of the criminal nature of the incident and held that while no data subjects were known to have suffered any pecuniary damage this was not a pre-condition for imposing a fine.[lxix]

Journalist Ingrid Lunden reported more insights into the incident:

From what we understand, some £150 million of the reduction was made as the ICO pieced apart the events that led to the attack and put less blame on BA than it had originally made; another £6 million was discounted based on BA's response, and a further £4 million was taken off as part of the ICO's COVID-19 policy, reflecting the impact the coronavirus pandemic has had on BA's business.

That step down underscores the impact the coronavirus pandemic is having on regulations. In some cases, in order to more quickly address issues that potentially impact business growth, we've seen regulators try to speed up their responsiveness to casework and even leave behind some previous reservations to green light activities, as in the case of e-scooters.

But in the case of the BA fine, we're seeing the other side of the COVID-19 impact: Regulators have chosen to take a less hard line when it comes to financial penalties when the company in question is already struggling. That could change the impact and also set a precedent in terms of how regulators respond to future cases of security and data protection neglect.[lxx]

During the height of the COVID-19 crisis the ICO announced very few fines but it continued to take some action, such as fining[lxxi] the transgender charity Mermaids 3% of its turnover for failing to keep the personal data of its users secure.

The ICO's investigation began after it received a data breach report from the charity in relation to an internal email group it set up and used from August 2016 until July 2017 when it was decommissioned. The charity only became aware of the breach in June 2019. The ICO found that the email group was created with insufficiently secure settings, which resulted in approximately 780 pages of confidential emails to be viewable online for nearly three years. This led to personal information, such as names and email addresses, of 550 people being searchable online. The personal data of 24 of those people was sensitive as it revealed how the person was coping and feeling, with a further 15 classified as special category data as mental and physical health and sexual orientation were exposed.

The ICO's investigation found Mermaids should have applied restricted access to its email group and could have considered pseudonymisation or encryption to add an extra layer of protection to the personal data it held. Under the UK GDPR, organisations that are responsible for personal data must ensure they have the appropriate technical and organisational measures in place to ensure personal data is secure. All decent DPOs should read this decision, as it shows the ICO's traditional enforcement approach, clearly identifying the infringement rather than just the incident that was reported to them.

In considering whether to take appropriate enforcement action against an organisation, the ICO will review the technical and organisational measures that organisations have put in place to address 'data protection by design and default' obligations. Instead of a fine, the ICO could issue an Enforcement Notice for any failings.[lxxii] Decent DPOs shouldn't hold out for an Enforcement Notice. Get your organisation to pay the fine. Enforcement Notices aren't any easier to manage than fines as they extend the engagement period with the ICO. With a fine, the direct engagement with the

ICO ends as soon as the fine is paid, and the ICO offers a 20% discount to prompt payers. With an enforcement notice, which typically requires specific measures to be taken within a specific time, the engagement will only end when the ICO is satisfied that the required actions have been taken. This extends the direct engagement with the ICO for, potentially, many months.

Decent DPOs will appreciate how challenging it is for data protection supervisory authorities to advocate relevant data protection standards in a constantly changing world. In an interview with journalist Catherine Stupp in September 2021, the then Information Commissioner Elizabeth Denham acknowledged the problem: *It's always difficult for lawmakers to keep up as technology changes and the pandemic has just accelerated the innovation and the uptake in digital services. It's accelerated beyond where we would have ever thought it would be at this point.* On the issue of tacking modern privacy problems, Denham considered that: *regulators, policy makers and privacy experts will need to devise new methods to better investigate companies. The current system is too slow, and mutual legal assistance treaties—the legal agreements allowing law enforcement authorities to share data with other countries—are cumbersome tools.* lxxiii

Decent DPOs don't rely on every piece of advice that is uttered by staff working for data protection supervisory authorities. Regulatory opinions are what they say they are – only opinions. Ultimately, only the courts can determine the true extent of privacy law. Decent DPOs develop their own ethical approach to key issues of the day, and then sell this approach to the organisation. I'll say more about this in my letter on teamwork.

Proposals to change UK data protection law in 2021

In September 2021 the UK Government consulted on changes to data protection law. Behind the scenes, an informed source advised me that the "ultra-remainiac ICO" had lobbied desperately hard to persuade officials at the Department of Digital, Culture, Media & Sport (DCMS, the Government department sponsoring the work of the ICO) that the UK should remain wedded to the European Union's data protection orthodoxy after leaving the Union, for fear of losing its data protection adequacy status. The lobbying efforts failed. The consultation paper[lxxiv] explained that the Government's overall aim was to alleviate some of the more prescriptive GDPR obligations on business, whilst retaining a robust data protection regime built largely on existing laws. This would evidently drive economic growth and innovation and strengthen public trust in use of data.

The outcome of the consultation exercise will not be known before I complete these letters, but decent DPOs will need to be aware of the key proposals,[lxxv] which have been reviewed by data protection lawyer Ruth Boardman and data protection trainer Chris Pounder. According to Boardman:

Some are small changes and clarifications intended to resolve uncertainties in the EU General Data Protection Regulation's drafting, while others are fundamental reforms to the operation of the U.K.'s data protection laws and the obligations and protections they bring. All organisations operating in the U.K. should be interested in potential changes to:

- *Data subject rights (to make them less burdensome).*
- *Accountability (potentially burdensome).*
- *Data transfers (significantly more flexibility).*
- *E-privacy (possibly helpful, although proposals not clearly articulated).*

There are also proposals of significant interest to those involved in research and AI, and reforms on the powers and governance of the Information Commissioner's Office, the supervisory authority. The proposed changes would significantly change the U.K.'s data protection landscape. Some of this would be welcome while other proposals are problematic or unclear. [lxxvi]

Pounder's, analysis, on the other hand, is gloomier: *The consultation's arguments for change are wholly unconvincing and there are significant errors in its analysis. Additionally, European Commission awarded the UK an adequacy agreement on the assumption that GDPR accountability standards would be maintained; they are not.* [lxxvii]

Data subject rights

Data Subject Access Requests changes

The consultation paper explained that the stated purpose of a Data Subject Access Request is to give individuals access to a copy of their personal data so they can *'be aware and verify the lawfulness of processing,'* although many organisations might question if this is really why some submit requests. The paper recognised the burden that responding to DSARs has on organisations, especially smaller businesses which often lack the resources to handle them. The possibility of reintroducing a nominal fee was raised. The consultation paper also proposed that the threshold for judging when a request may be vexatious / manifestly unfounded be amended.

Boardman commented: *This proposal will be welcomed by controllers in the U.K. Many organisations have felt the burden of "weaponised DSARs" and the introduction of a cost limit would reduce this burden. The suggestion made by DCMS is that this should be based on the existing and well-established regime under the Freedom of Information Act, which allows public authorities to refuse freedom of information requests that cost more than £450-600 (depending on the type of organisation). A sliding scale depending on turnover and sector may be a good model.*[lxxviii]

Data breach notification threshold changes

Thanks to the GDPR, data protection supervisory authorities have been inundated with data breach reports. It is not surprising that organisations over-report when they face a legal obligation for to report a personal breach if it is likely to represent a 'risk' to individuals.

The consultation paper proposed that organisations would only need to report a personal data breach where the risk to the individual is 'material'. The ICO would be encouraged to produce clear guidance and examples of what would be 'non-material' risk, and what would or would not be considered a reportable breach. Pounder agrees: *The way to overcome the problem of over reporting data breaches to the ICO is for the ICO improve her guidance. There is no need to raise the threshold of data breach reporting so that only "material" impacts on individuals are reported.*[lxxix]

<u>Accountability</u>

No mandatory Data Protection Officers

My letter on education will explain that DPOs must be appointed by public authorities and in the commercial sector if organisations meet specific criteria. The GDPR also sets out specific requirements and responsibilities for the role. The consultation paper proposed that the requirement for a DPO be replaced with a requirement to designate a suitable individual (or individuals) responsible for overseeing compliance. However, the new law wouldn't lay down specific requirements & obligations for this role.

Pounder is extremely concerned at this proposal:

The Consultation makes several mistakes and omissions when explaining its DPO proposals. It follows that if its arguments are misleading then its conclusions are suspect, then DPO removal or reduction cannot be justified in terms of the official reasons provided by the Consultation.

The Consultation states that the private sector needs a DPO when "certain types of processing" occur (para 161). A precise (and less sinister) description of these "certain types of processing" would refer to "core activities" that involve the processing of "large scale" special category of personal data or "large scale" criminal offence personal data, or involve systematic or regular surveillance of data subjects on a "large scale".

The omission of "large scale" and "core activities" plus the use of "certain types of processing" suggest to the reader that more DPOs are needed when, in practice, the current statutory requirement for a DPO is relatively limited. The Consultation does not provide one example of a DPO being appointed when there was no statutory requirement to appoint one. Important evidence to support the proposed changes is therefore missing.

The Consultation then goes on to state that "Some organisations may struggle to appoint an individual with the requisite skills and who is sufficiently independent from other duties, especially in the case of smaller organisations" and as a result "The government therefore proposes to remove the existing requirements to designate a data protection officer" (para 162-163).

*There are at least two things wrong with these two statements. "Smaller private organisations" would need a DPO **only** if they were engaged, for example, in large scale and systematic surveillance or the processing of large scale criminal records or health data and these were "core activities".*

*Such small organisations, I contend, **do not exist** in large numbers; the Consultation gives the impression they do. It is noteworthy that the Consultation does not provide a single example of any such small organisation.*

Secondly, when there is a shortage of DPO skills, the Consultation proposes to do away the requirement to have a DPO.

This argument is wholly specious. For example, does the Government solve the shortage of HGV drivers (or brain surgeons or whatever) by removing the obligation to have the "requisite skills" to become an HGV driver (or brain surgeon or whatever)?

In general, I suspect the need for the appointment of a DPO in the private sector has been worded in order to provide the answer the Government wants: that many controllers will strongly agree that DPOs are not needed (even though the respondents themselves don't have to appoint a DPO).

Finally, the idea to abolish DPOs on the basis of a skills shortage shows that how low the Government values the skills of the data protection profession.[lxxx]

I say more about this issue, and will outline the ICO's response to the proposal, in my letter on career development.

No mandatory requirement for Data Protection Impact Assessments

My letter on accepting risks explained that Data Protection Impact Assessments are mandatory for high-risk activities. The GDPR also sets out core elements such an assessment must include and requires supervisory authorities to establish a list of processing operations which definitely require a DPIA. The consultation paper proposed to remove this mandatory requirement. Don't think this means dispensing with screening questionnaires and DPIA templates, as these are often very useful. The onus would be on your organisation to take a proportionate and risk-based decision on **when** to carry out impact assessments and **how** to go about this.

As far as Pounder is concerned: *the proposed change is likely to protect controllers that adopt a lackadaisical approach to risk assessment.*[lxxxi]

More flexible record keeping

Completing and maintaining up-to-date records, known as Records of Processing Activities (ROPA) is one of the more onerous tasks that a DPO must oversee. The GDPR and the guidance from data protection supervisory authorities is prescriptive about records keeping requirements – although small and medium sized organisations (with less than 250 employees) are supposed to be exempt from this. The consultation paper proposed a more flexible model for record keeping.

Maintaining a central record of what personal data your organisation holds, what it's used for, where it's stored and who it's shared with is a useful asset. Many records management professionals feel such records are vital to effective data risk management. So, you may not need to rip up your current ROPA, but the proposals would allow your organisation to adapt your record keeping practices to suit your specific needs and perhaps make the records easier to maintain.

Pounder is unhappy with the proposal: *A ROPA under A.30(1) requires the controller to compile an inventory of **all** the controller's processing which is couched in data protection terms (e.g. an inventory of the controller's processing purposes, recipients, transfers, retention times, security arrangements, and a description of the personal data processed).*

***All** processing purposes have to be described in the controller's ROPA. If the processing is not described in a ROPA it is tantamount to the admission that the controller is not wholly in control of all the processing of personal data. That is why ROPA forms part of the accountability arrangements; accountable processing is that described in a ROPA.*

The Consultation is not getting rid of the need for an inventory, as inventories forms part of the proposed privacy management programme. However, as each controller can decide what to put into its own inventory, there is a significant risk is that inventories become inconsistent across all controllers (e.g. one bank's inventory might be different to that of another bank).[lxxxii]

Accountability & Privacy Management Programmes (PMPs)

Changes to the accountability framework were proposed, with businesses expected to have a Privacy Management Programme in place. The consultation paper argued this would allow organisations ignore some of the more burdensome accountability obligations that had been imposed by the GDPR and permit them to implement a risk-based privacy programme based on the volume and sensitivity of personal data they handle and the types of activities they're involved in. Your organisation would still need to know where the data is, what it is used for, implement robust security measures, manage suppliers, assess privacy risks and fulfil privacy rights, but there could be more flexibility and control over how this is achieved.

This would not mean throwing away all the hard work your organisation has already done to comply with GDPR. Many DPOs may choose to remain with the tried and tested framework they've already established. Others may use this opportunity to adapt their approach. UK organisations operating in Europe will still be governed by EU GDPR, so they will be less able to take advantage of the opportunity to make changes.

Boardman commented: *The departure from the existing GDPR framework for accountability is puzzling. DCMS's stated reason for the proposed reform is that current accountability obligations place a "disproportionate administrative burden" on organizations, yet its proposals involve replacing existing accountability requirements with other very similar (and no less burdensome) obligations. With the exception of the higher threshold for breach reporting, all other accountability requirements have been replaced with a different compliance requirement, often with the choice of the format left to organisations. This would likely create more work for organisations, which would need to assess whether their existing GDPR documentation matched the new U.K. requirements. For example, there is a suggestion that GDPR data protection officers could not serve as the person responsible for the privacy management program (as the independence they require for GDPR purposes would — implicitly — disqualify them from this new role), so that an organisation that chose to retain its DPO would need to appoint an additional data protection professional (164). The proposals seem to diverge from the GDPR without providing any discernible benefit to organizations in the U.K.*

Data transfers

In the wake of "Schrems II" and the associated EDPB guidance from the European Data Protection Board, transferring data out of the EU and U.K. has been much more complicated. The consultation paper proposed a number of reforms to improve the U.K. aspect of this, from encouraging adoption of existing mechanisms (use of codes of conduct) to widening existing mechanisms (such as the derogations under Article 49 GDPR). The consultation paper also included a more controversial proposal to allow exporters to make their own decisions about how to protect personal data being transferred out of the U.K., including by using contracts developed by the contracting parties without the ICO's review or approval. Boardman commented: *This proposal is based on the approach taken in New Zealand and was possible in the U.K. under the Data Protection Act 1998.*[lxxxiii]

Changes to ePrivacy

Headlines surrounding ePrivacy reform usually focus on ending the barrage of cookie pop-ups. The consultation paper proposed two main options:

- permitting organisations to use analytics cookies and similar technologies without the user's consent. In other words, treating them in the same way as 'strictly necessary' cookies. This proposal is included in the most recent EU ePrivacy draft. Further safeguards would be required to ensure this had a negligible impact on user privacy and any risk of harm. The proposal would also not absolve organisations from providing clear and comprehensive information about cookies and similar technologies; or

- permitting organisations to store information on, or collect information from, a user's device without their consent for other limited purposes. An example given is that this could include processing necessary for the legitimate interests of controllers where the impact on privacy is likely to be minimal.

Extended use of the 'soft opt-in'

The consultation paper explained that PECR currently permits email and SMS marketing messages where consent has been given, or for existing customers only, when the soft opt-in requirements are met. This exemption to consent for existing customers is only currently available to commercial organisations. It was proposed that this could be extended to other organisations such as political parties and charities.

Boardman commented: *The consultation has widely been announced as a reform of the U.K. GDPR, yet a section on the U.K.'s Privacy and Electronic Communications Regulations has also been included. Most changes in this area are relatively minor and are likely to be welcomed both by controllers and data subjects. There is an attempt to obtain cross-party support for at least some of the proposals by proposing to exempt political parties from these rules in their entirety, although the consultation document does acknowledge that the prospect of receiving automated calls from political parties may not be welcomed by everyone.*

The proposal also includes a call for views on how organisations could comply with the GDPR's principles of lawfulness, fairness and transparency "without use of the cookie pop-up notices." This section references browser settings as a possible option but offers no other suggestions, so it is hard to assess the possible impact of this. [lxxxiv]

Research and reuse of data

In line with the U.K. government's National Data Strategy, the consultation paper proposed reforms to encourage research in the U.K. The paper stressed that data protection laws are complex and difficult to navigate, which discourages researchers from using personal data.

Boardman commented: *The proposal to consolidate all research-specific data protection provisions may achieve the aim of bringing greater clarity to the area, though it is unlikely to have a strong impact. The proposal also suggests moving a number of research-related recitals into the Articles of the U.K. GDPR to increase legal certainty. As part of this, the U.K. GDPR would define scientific research in law, and the consultation seeks views as to what this should be defined as.*

There is also a proposal to include a new legal basis for scientific research under Article 6 U.K. GDPR, to match the condition for processing sensitive personal data for research purposes under Article 9. Currently, researchers would be likely to rely on either research being necessary for a task in the public interest or necessary for a legitimate interest, so it is unclear what benefit this would bring; further, to the extent clarity could help, it could be achieved by guidance instead of primary legislation.

Much of the discussion on research focuses on challenges faced by universities. The private sector is also a critical part of the U.K. research base and it would be advisable for private sector organizations engaging in research to make clear to DCMS that their interests must also be considered.

The consultation includes a number of proposals on how to change the law relating to reuse of data for research purposes. The proposals in this area are not wholly clear and are in some cases contradictory. They include clarifying that a broad consent is permitted when obtaining consent for research and that reuse for research is always compatible with the original purpose, both of which would be welcome but could be achieved by regulatory guidance rather than new legislation.

There are also (unclear) proposals to allow further processing for incompatible purposes when this safeguards an important public interest (54). The Data Protection Act 2018 already allows this for the public interest purposes specified in Schedule 2. Allowing a general public interest override to purpose limitation will significantly weaken protections for individuals, so it would be useful to understand the size of the problem that DCMS thinks it is addressing with this proposal.

It is also striking that the consultation does not make any reference to the laws relating to patient confidentiality beyond data protection law. In the authors' experience, it is the law in this area which is the biggest constraint on research — both as a matter of principle and because of uncertainty in interpretation. No amount of tidying up data protection law will achieve significant benefit unless this is addressed.[lxxxv]

Legitimate interests

The consultation paper proposed to create an exhaustive list of legitimate interests which organisations could rely on without needing to conduct the balancing test, i.e. no Legitimate Interest Assessment (LIA) required. as the legislation would recognise the processing purposes as always outweighing the interests of the individuals. The following examples were given:

- ensuring bias monitoring, detection and correction in AI systems
- statutory public communications and public health & safety messages by non-public bodies
- network security
- internal research and development projects

Where an activity was not on the list, presumably assessments using the current 3-step test would still be needed.

Boardman commented: *The proposed list is relatively limited and uncontroversial and would helpfully reduce the burden of documentation obligations.*[lxxxvi]

Artificial Intelligence & machine learning

The consultation paper proposed that certain automated decision-making should be permitted without human oversight. The GDPR prohibits this unless necessary for a contract with an individual, authorised by law or based on explicit consent. Ruth Boardman commented: *The consultation document notes that "currently, an AI practitioner needs to consider each use case individually and work out each time whether the data protection regime permits the activities." Our view is that this statement not only holds true of any processing activity in any industry but is true of other legal considerations outside of data protection. The application of the law is always based on the relevant facts and consequentially, new projects will require new assessments of the law.*

The proposal to reform the law to make the use of sensitive personal data for bias detection and correction easier is likely unnecessary. The existing framework under the U.K. GDPR and Data Protection Act permits this, and the ICO has already provided sector-specific guidance in this area.

The proposal to support the development and use of data intermediaries could be very beneficial to organizations sharing data for research and development purposes. Though the consultation document is very light on detail in this area, the proposal is welcome and could allow for innovative frameworks for data sharing within the existing data protection framework.

The proposal has an interesting discussion of algorithmic "fairness" — it postulates that determination of what is fair should be best left to sector-specific regulators rather than the ICO (79).

It also suggests clarifying when data will be regarded as "anonymous." The suggestions to write Recital 26 into the text of U.K. GDPR seem to add little to current guidance from the ICO on this topic. More interestingly, DCMS suggests it may stipulate that anonymization should be assessed based on whether it is likely that the controller can identify the data subject. This would be a more permissive test than that set out in the GDPR, which requires one to consider the likelihood of identification by the controller or by another person (i.e., by anyone). In effect, this would be a return to the provisions of the Data Protection Act 1998. The proposal would help to clarify that if party A releases deidentified data to party B but retains the underlying identifiable data, the fact that party A could still identify individuals in the data would not automatically result in the data being personal in party B's hands. Currently, if data is made accessible to the public at large (rather than a limited group of recipients), it is typical to require a higher standard of deidentification to achieve anonymization, as it is harder to assess the motives and means an unknown actor may have to identify the data. It is not clear how the proposal would protect individuals in this situation.[lxxxvii]

Reform of the ICO

The consultation paper proposed that the ICO be given stronger enforcement powers and longer timelines for enforcement action. Boardman commented: *The extension of the limitation period for investigations in particular will give the ICO more time to assess whether or not to issue a notice, potentially increasing the number of notices issued. The proposals are not disproportionate and are likely to have a beneficial impact on the regulatory environment in the U.K.*[lxxxviii]

The consultation paper proposes substantial amendments to the ICO's internal governance and relationship with its sponsoring department, DCMS. Decent DPOs can ignore these proposals as they would not directly impact their compliance obligations. Highlights are:

- the move away from a corporation sole (the Information Commissioner) to a more corporate model, where the commissioner would be the chair of the ICO with a separate CEO;

- ICO to take over the role of the Biometrics Commissioner and the Surveillance Camera Commissioner;

- a statutory framework that sets out the ICO's strategic objectives (suggested as upholding data rights and encouraging trustworthy and responsible data use) and priorities;

- an express obligation to consider the desirability of promoting economic growth (already relevant under the Deregulation Act 2015), to consider the impact of its activities on competition and on public safety, and a statutory obligation to share data with some other regulators, including the Competition and Markets Authority;

- ICO would have to adopt and report against key performance indicators (for those frustrated by delays to binding corporate rules approvals, perhaps this could be suggested?); and

- lessening the obligation on the ICO to deal with low-level complaints and for this to be replaced by an obligation on controllers to have published complaints policies and to publish information on the number and type of complaints received.

Pounder is not happy: *Make no bones about it: the proposals for "Reform of the Information Commissioner's Office" comprise a power grab to influence (or determine) what the Commissioner's duties and priorities should be. The independence of the UK's data protection regulator is wholly undermined by these proposals. This has the potential to have a knock-on effect with respect to the Adequacy Agreement signed with the European Commission.*[lxxxix]

Even if all these proposals were to be incorporated into English law, In my view it is unlikely that the UK would become the 'Wild West' for data, as some people may fear. The Government clearly hopes any changes will be broadly compatible with EU equivalency, enabling the UK to continue to exchange personal data with the EU as it currently does.

DPOs will always be concerned at the implications of EC adequacy decisions being held over the UK Government like the Sword of Damocles, as the withdrawal of an adequacy determination will require every UK organisation to carry out yet another repapering exercise with EU-based organisations to ensure that personal data continues to flow across borders. In my judgement, that sword is unlikely to fall should these changes be made to the UK's Data Protection Act. But, as I'll explain in my letter on international privacy issues, a determination of EU adequacy is just as much a political decision on the part of the EU as it is a legal decision.

Whether the Government's proposals to reform data protection laws will do more harm than good is an open question. Time will tell. What you can be certain of is that the legislation that is currently on the statute book will, in due course, change. And, later, it will change again. Decent DPOs prepare their organisations for a world of constant change.

7 OVERWHELMING WORKLOADS

In my letter on doing the right thing, I referred to psychologist Oliver Burkeman's comment that *there will always be too much to do – and this realisation is liberating.* There's no reason for you to assume that there will be any fit between the demands on your time – all the things you would like to do or feel you ought to do – and the amount of time available. These demands will keep increasing, while your capacities will remain largely fixed. It follows that the attempt to "get on top of everything" is doomed. Indeed, it's worse than that – the more tasks you get done, the more you'll generate.

The upside is that you needn't berate yourself for failing to do it all, since doing it all is impossible. The only viable solution is to make a shift: from a life spent trying not to neglect anything, to one spent proactively and consciously choosing what to neglect, in favour of what matters most.

Don't be surprised if your senior management team lacks a true appreciation of the tasks that a DPO is accountable for. Job descriptions based on the requirements set out in the GDPR will set out little more than a high-level summary of a DPO's true role profile. You should expect your own responsibilities to change as your organisation's data protection compliance programme matures.

Take this example of a DPO's evolving role profile, as imagined by the DPO Centre:

Meet Alison Jones – Early in her privacy career

Three years ago, Alison worked with the compliance team. She'd left university with a good law degree and had managed several projects, some of them IT based. With the upcoming introduction of the GDPR, her manager asked her if she could find out more about what was involved and how it would impact her organisation.

What did they need do to? She soon realised she needed to become a GDPR subject matter expert (SME) and enrolled on a Certified Information Privacy Professional Europe (CIPP/E) training course.

Understanding the GDPR – Alison the Translator

Very quickly Alison was seen as the GDPR specialist. Her first job was to translate the regulation into words the rest of the company could understand. She interpreted the legalese and explained in practice what her business should do to comply. She did this for every department handling personal data - whether it was human resources, finance, sales and marketing, operations or IT and tried to cut through the GDPR hype appearing in the press.

Of course, she didn't fully understand how each different department used personal data or the processes and procedures they used, so she needed to learn how things worked in her company and then identify how the GDPR should be applied.

Enforcing the GDPR – Police Officer Alison

Alison quickly realised there were potential issues across the business. Like many organisations, the company often treated personal data as its own. Several well-established processes were clearly not compliant. Alison was often seen to be, "getting in the way of things". Sometimes she felt like a broken record and was frequently heard to utter phrases like "we can't keep this data anymore", "we need a lawful basis for that", "we need to put an appropriate policy in place".

Ultimately her main task was to make sure the organisation wasn't exposed to unnecessary risk, particularly given the greater powers of the ICO and the new potential of significantly increased financial penalties. Alison needed persistence, a sense of humour and thick skin. Whilst she always tried to explain her thinking and provide constructive solutions, some senior managers and staff were very resistant to change.

Making things happen – Alison the Change Agent

Gradually, persistence began to pay off. With support from an increasing number of the senior management team and aided by some well publicised actions by the ICO (notably British Airways, Marriott and Cambridge Analytica) Alison began to make people realise the importance of changing to comply with the GDPR.

To be effective, Alison had to combine her technical legal skills with an understanding of the commercial needs of the organisation and the market it operates in. Much of her time was taken training and raising awareness with staff about their new responsibilities and how and why they needed to do things differently. When trying to change business processes that didn't comply, she found she was trying to apply influence with limited authority – something that's never easy. She had to develop her soft skills as well as her technical ones and became a great communicator and diplomat. However, when push came to shove, she was never shy to wield the 'big stick' of the law and potential penalties to assist with her persuasion!

Moving centre stage – Alison the Strategist

Looking back over the last 3 years, Alison's DPO role has changed dramatically. Having started off with the simple task of being asked to find out more about the GDPR before it came into force, she's had to be a translator, an enforcer and then help facilitate and influence huge amounts of change across all areas of the business.

She's written policies, put processes and procedures in place to monitor data protection compliance and mitigate risks. She's helped map personal data across the organisation, she ensures Records of Processing Activities are in place, that Subject Access Requests are answered and that individuals can exercise their rights under data protection law. She's trained employees about their responsibilities and worked with third parties to put data processing and sharing agreements in place to make sure appropriate safeguards have been implemented.

As more and more personal data is processed digitally and migrated to the cloud, the lines between data protection and information security are becoming increasingly blurred, so now she's working more closely with the IT and cyber security team. She's answering directly to senior management and her opinion is sought when designing and implementing new business systems and processes. Increasingly she's moving centre stage and involved in higher level strategic discussions.[xc]

As the DPO, your daily work is likely to include most the following areas:

- monitoring the progress of your organisation's accountability programme;
- advising on tricky subject access requests (i.e. deciding what personal data should be provided and what should be redacted);
- handling data protection complaints (e.g. regarding the accuracy of personal data, data being shared with people that the individual didn't want it to be shared with);
- dealing with requests for personal data from third party organisations (e.g. the police, insurance companies or solicitors);
- drafting – or at least advising on – privacy policies and fair processing statements;
- carrying out data protection impact assessments on a new project or initiatives;
- reviewing personal data security incidents; and

- liaising with the Information Commissioner's Office.

This is a lot to cover and it's not for those that lack confidence in themselves. Don't get too downhearted, though. In July 2021, an unhappy privacy professional tweeted about her own situation: *I am an abject failure as a DPO. Shit hot at DSAR trouble shooting, still drowning and unable to even chip at improvement. Doing nothing except fucking firefighting is getting me down.*[xci] Her tweet led to the following sympathetic response: *I know this may sound trite, but while it is important work, it is only work, and your mental health is worth more than that.*[xcii]

Don't view each day with dread. It's just not worth it. I do know how you can feel, though. As comedian Russell Brand observed: *my mum worked hard to make my birthdays jolly, but they were always a right stomach-churning drag.*[xciii] Instead, do what you can to abandon the impossible and push back against what the American writer Marilynne Robinson has called the *joyless urgency* of our age.[xciv]

Try to resolve not to reply too quickly to emails, as it only generates more traffic and often the impending crisis flagged up by the sender just goes away anyway.

Psychologist Burkeman diagnoses the modern condition as *existential overwhelm*. There are just far too many things that seem worth doing. You should embrace *the joy of missing out*: the recognition that renouncing alternatives is what makes any choice meaningful. We should surrender to what Germans call *Eigenzeit*, the time integral to a process itself. If a thing's worth doing, it takes as long as it takes.

Burkeman urges everyone to accept the *blunt but unexpectedly liberating truth: that what you do with your life doesn't matter all that much.* [xcv]

As a DPO, you're likely at times to suffer stress, anxiety, isolation and despair. Accordingly, it is extremely important that you do what you can to find time to improve your overall life satisfaction, happiness, life being worthwhile and anxiety levels.

What does it feel like to have a breakdown? Former corporate high-flier and founder of the charity Minds@Work Geoff McDonald describes himself as a successful midlife man who became overwhelmed by life yet didn't have the tools to recognise what was happening:

The tingling had been spreading through my fingers for a few minutes by the time my heart started to pound vigorously. I was struggling to breathe; my chest felt like it was closing in. My bed sheets were wet with sweat. Gasping, I told my wife I was having a heart attack. She asked me to walk slowly around the bedroom, taking deep breaths. I obliged, and once my breathing was under control I returned to bed. I was left staring at the ceiling, wondering what exactly had just happened.

I was 46 in January 2008 when, out of the blue, that episode struck. Being a HR executive on a six-figure salary at Unilever required hard work and long hours, and I was a husband and father of two young girls – life had its stresses, yet it wasn't unmanageable, I thought.

But my symptoms at our Surrey home that night were, I would later learn, typical of a panic attack. An emotional breakdown, as some might describe it. It's not something I ever believed would happen to me: I was raised in South Africa in the 1960s and 1970s, an era when men were not encouraged to dwell on their feelings. My mother taught me the importance of dental hygiene, but never the importance of emotional welfare.

Former Doctor Who actor Christopher Eccleston, 57, opened up that he too "nearly lost everything" during his emotional breakdown in 2016, which saw him admitted to hospital with clinical depression. "There was one night I thought I was going to die. I was running down Euston Road [in London] with a suitcase. If anybody had seen me they'd have gone, 'Oh, there's Doctor Who'. I don't think people understand how quickly it can happen."

For men, there seems to be something about midlife that makes once-bearable strains feel overwhelming. Work and family pressures combine, amplifying one another. Three times as many men as women die by suicide in the UK, according to the Mental Health Foundation, with men in their 40s the worst affected group.

The day after my panic attack, I visited my GP. I expected him to take my temperature, or check my heart rate. Instead, he asked how I was feeling. "Anxiety-induced depression" was his diagnosis. It came as a horrible shock. But if I'd been better informed about mental illness, it wouldn't have been a surprise at all. In retrospect, I can see that for four or five weeks before the panic attack I hadn't been in a good place. I was much more irritable than normal — something so banal as not having a seat on a train would make me unreasonably frustrated; I would catastrophise over the smallest things, believing a cold sore was mouth cancer.

I started waking at 3am, worrying about work and finances, and would climb out of bed without feeling much like breakfast. I stopped reading newspapers: a sad story would trigger my anxiety. I stopped looking forward to my Saturday morning bicycle ride with friends; warning lights I was too ignorant to notice.

My depression diagnosis felt like a liberation. Finally, my feelings made sense. My company gave me three months off work. At first, I was wracked with guilt; I felt like I'd failed. For a long time I struggled to get out of bed each morning, and the negativity of everything in my head became self-perpetuating. I felt lonely and worthless, and would spend days doing nothing, just ruminating and catastrophising when I would have otherwise been working a full day at a major international firm — which only seemed to reinforce how useless I had convinced myself I was. I was aggrieved, too: why had this happened to me? When would I feel better? Why weren't things improving more quickly? At my lowest, I was suicidal, so certain that I was a burden to those around me that my absence would be better.

Being frank about what I was going through was hard, but when I explained my situation to those closest to me, I was touched. Family and friends explained how much they loved me – knowing that saved me in my darkest moments. So too did a sense of hope.

With the help of therapy and antidepressants, I started on a robust road to recovery – it began with waking up one morning a week feeling good, then twice, then three times. I got back on my bike, and wanted to go for a run, and see friends again. Still, I remember the fear of walking over Blackfriars Bridge into my glass-walled office on that first morning back at work, unsure of how I would be received. But everything seemed to get better as time went on, aside from a brief relapse in 2010 (which was nowhere near as bad as my first depressive spell). I assumed the worst was behind me.

Two years later, I received a phone call from Debbie, my wife. "Something terrible has happened," she said. One of my friends, a South African father of three, had just taken his own life. He was the most fun-loving, energetic and compassionate person. The brighter the light, the darker the shadow.

I was devastated. That night I lay in bed thinking about him. He clearly hadn't felt able to confide in me. What if he had? What if he'd spoken to more people about his feelings? I'm not saying he'd definitely still be alive – suicide is complex. But even if there was just the tiniest chance that a conversation might have saved him, wasn't that worth exploring?

That evening I emailed [journalist] Alistair Campbell, who has spoken about his own experience of depression in midlife. He replied within 10 minutes, explaining that he wanted more senior people to share their experiences in the corporate world – a place where many people suffer, but few speak out. I feel indebted to Alastair; he helped me take my first tiny steps on my journey to eradicate the stigma of mental ill-health. And so, almost by accident, my friend's tragedy ended up being the catalyst that contributed to me leaving my job and setting up my charity, Minds@Work, with my co-founder Georgie Mack.

Today I tour workplaces and across the world – banks, law firms, advertising companies, the civil service – speaking on the importance of mental health. I've discovered there's an undiagnosed epidemic in the corporate world. The main issues are burnout, depression and anxiety. I want to help companies to elevate employee wellbeing to a strategic priority and teach employees to spot the warning signs.

My work moved online during the pandemic, and I was overwhelmed by just how many employees across the world – many of them successful middle-aged men, as I had been when my breakdown struck – were suffering immensely under Covid. Economic uncertainty, home-schooling and the inability to see friends and family were clearly taking a dreadful toll.

I can only hope that talking more openly about the difficulties we face will help turn the tide. Speaking to employees about it and trying to be a role model to my daughters is now my main focus: I want them to know they have a mother and father who truly understand them, and that there's no stigma in our family. It's the least I can do for them, and the least I can do for my much-missed friend.

There are ways to ensure that DPOs can cope with the stresses of modern life. Are the material benefits that DPOs enjoy worth the attendant psychological pressures the role brings? Journalist John Armstrong has his own ideas on regaining calm and wisdom:

Work/life balance

One of the most pernicious ideas of modern times is that of work/life balance. In an age when the historic division between 'breadwinners' and 'homemakers' has broken down, it is possible – even easy – to have both a successful career and a successful home life. Yet this is a fallacy: one ensured by our modern conceptions of what 'success' means in both contexts. In the business world, where competition, tight deadlines and constant communication are the norm, we must be prepared to work punishingly long hours to scale the heights of the ladder. At the same time, we have massively raised our expectations of what marriage and parenting consist of: our partners and children must have all our time, attention and affection if they are to remain healthy and content.

The solution is to surrender the expectation of achieving a work/life balance. This isn't to say that homemakers can't hold down jobs, or that professionals should give up on household chores. It's to accept that those who choose to focus on their careers will almost certainly have deficiencies as partners and parents, while those who orient themselves around family shouldn't castigate themselves for failing to become CEOs. We need to make peace with whatever imbalance we choose to strike.

Consumerism

We have become a consumer society. In the past, the route to happiness ran through immaterial concepts: through loving God, serving a master or performing our role in a rigid social hierarchy. In contrast, our secular, capitalist society promises a single remedy for all our ills: shopping. The things we buy aren't simply meant to perform a function: they have the power to make us happy. The solution to our misery is simply a question of what brand of car or laundry detergent we should purchase.

The issue isn't so much with the idea of materialism per se. It has much more to do with our illiteracy around our own emotional needs. The modern world teaches us next to nothing about what we, ourselves, actually need to be happy. A better route lies in self-knowledge: thoroughly examining our thoughts, memories and feelings for clues as to what our lives are missing.

Busy-ness

It is no surprise that our society is 'busier' than the last. One of the hallmarks of the modern age has been the rise of productivity. In historical terms, we make more things much faster than ever before. This trend has led to our making a virtue of activity for activity's sake. In the modern view, unless we are constantly, ceaselessly 'busy', we must be wasting time.

This notion isn't only making us unmanageably tired and stressed, it's preventing us from seeing the very real benefits inactivity can offer. Moments of supposed 'laziness' – relaxing in a bath or staring out of a window – are often when our minds are at their most productive. To become more efficient (and less stressed), we need to give ourselves permission to be lazy.

Meritocracy

In the modern world, one's value is no longer determined by the place where one was born, or the class one belongs to. Instead, value is based on merit alone. It is our achievements that make us who we are.

The problem with this attractive-sounding idea is that it massively raises the spectre of failure. The pre-modern world didn't see moments of failure (which might be the result of a capricious God or fate) as a guide to one's worth as a person. Yet in a fully meritocratic world, success and failure are not accidents, but indicators of genuine value. To recover from setbacks, we should stop judging others – or ourselves – as either 'successes' or 'failures', since everyone is a mixture of both.

Progress

Perhaps the defining idea of the modern age is our belief in progress. Whereas the societies of the past emphasised tradition and continuity, we see progress (whether technological or moral) as both a necessary and desirable fact of life. Yet, taken to its logical extremes, the notion of progress presupposes the idea of perfection: an ideal end state towards which humanity is headed.

This cult of perfectionism is a modern phenomenon. In the past, religions like Christianity and Buddhism stressed the idea of man's essential frailty. We would do well to rehabilitate such notions. Perfection is impossible since all humans are, by definition, flawed and imperfect. We should abandon the cult of perfectionism and fashion a cult of imperfectionism in its place.[xcvi]

Be mindful of the cumulative effect of your organisation's standards and policies

As well as dealing with your own overwhelming workload, you should be mindful of the workloads carried by your co-workers. You should take care, when developing policies and standards, that the cumulative impact on your organisation's staff is not overwhelm your co-workers to the extent that they take deliberate steps to ignore them. Each fresh policy and standard represents an incremental burden on the compliance workload that every employee is expected to carry, usually unsupported and under what they may well perceive to be hostile scrutiny. Eventually, what you think of as a straw will be sufficient to break their back.

While I'm unaware of any academic research on the cumulative impact of complying with data protection rules, the latest research into the impacts of corporate security policies strongly suggests that organisations should not overburden staff with reams of detailed requirements:

Security mechanisms will not be effective if individual employees chose not to comply. Most employees will comply if this does not require any additional effort. When extra effort is required, individuals will weigh this extra effort against benefits for them, in the context of their production tasks. If their goals are aligned with the organisation's security goals, there is no conflict, as the behaviour required individual translates into perceived gain for them as well as for the organisation. Thus, security policies are likely to be followed – at least by most individuals, most of the time.

Conversely, most individuals will not be inclined to choose the behaviour required by the organisation if there is a conflict between the security behaviour and their own goals. In this case, either some part of the joint set of goals will not be met, and the individual to expend effort without gain to help the organisation's security goals.

Compliance is if the individual chooses the behaviour required by the organisation, even though it makes it harder for them to realise their goals, or even prevents them from reaching them altogether. Compliance can be seen as a kind of organisational altruism. From the individual's perspective, this is a situation of 'pain but no gain' (recall we are focusing on conflict situations where individual and organizational goals are unaligned). The 'pain tolerance' - the amount of extra effort an individual is prepared to make for no personal gain – is what we call the Compliance Budget. The limit of the Compliance Budget is referred to as the compliance threshold; this being the point at which the individual no longer has the will to comply with official requirements. The closer an individual is to his compliance threshold the higher the cost to the organisation of achieving compliance, as the perceived cost to the individual will also be higher. Once the compliance threshold has been exceeded, there will be almost no way to achieve compliance, except through heavy monitoring of individuals' behaviour, and enforcement.[xcvii]

Decent DPOs will aim to write short policies for their organisations. Some DPOs try to keep their policies to a single page. The shorter and clearer the document, the more likely it is that your organisation's HR colleagues, when taking disciplinary action against a fellow employee, will be able to argue that the offender must have known what your organisation's rules were.

.

8 TEAMWORK

You are not solely responsible for ensuring that your organisation adheres to its data protection obligations. Even if you are the only person with data protection responsibilities in their job description, it's vital to appreciate that whether your organisation likes it or not, you're going to need to work other people to help the organisation meet its obligations. Your key supporters will be:

- your senior management team, helping you developing a culture of 'privacy awareness' and ensuring your organisation develops decent data protection policies and procedures;
- your organisation's software engineers, system architects and application developers, i.e. those who design systems, products and services which take account of data protection requirements and assist you in complying with your obligations; and
- your organisation's customer support staff, the first people that customers will engage with.

Don't see yourself as a project or a change manager. You have an advice-giving, monitoring role, so if you're the sort of person who likes to focus on setting up structures and processes, you're probably not the right person to be a DPO. When organisations prepared for the coming into force of the General Data Protection Regulation, they needed programme managers to support the DPO. As they continued their compliance journey, many organisations realised the value of good change managers. Embedding GDPR-compliant processes within an organisation is tough.

Given the frequency with which data protection laws rules change, you will almost certainly find yourself working closely with project or change managers to change your organisation's existing data protection practices to being them more into line with today's legal requirements. Whereas project management focusses on the processes and activities needed to complete a project (such as a new software application), change management focusses on the people affected by those projects (or other changes within an organisation).

You will need to exercise good teamwork skills. You can't expect to do all this stuff by yourself. The most effective programmes I've worked on were those where project managers worked closely with committed stakeholders from all parts of the organisation. I've been involved with many programmes that failed because key parts of the organisation refused to effectively engage with the project manager. I've had difficulties with legal and procurement teams when it became necessary to agree who was accountable for ensuring that supplier contracts contained the correct data protection clauses. I've also had difficulties getting process owners to agree who was accountable for documenting the personal data flows that are associated with their processes. The lack of engagement was usually because these colleagues did not have the resources to carry out what they saw as someone-else's data protection tasks, nor did they want to ask for the additional resources that would be required should they agree to perform them. This is a matter that programme managers exist to solve. Just make sure they get on and solve it.

The key problem has often been that senior managers have not determined with sufficient granularity who is accountable for doing what within their organisation. Despite the requirements of the General Data Protection Regulation,[xcviii] many DPOs have found it extremely challenging to get senior managers to properly appreciate what controls and what accountabilities should be in place. This leads to confusion and poor morale. Some people get upset because they feel required to do more work than they are officially recognised as being responsible for. Their frustration mounts when others don't step up to the mark when they should.

I've had particularly strained relationships with colleagues with information security obligations. While privacy laws require your organisation to take appropriate measures to ensure the security of personal data, it has been challenging for most of the organisations I've worked with to determine precisely what measures should be in place and to get them in place. Sometimes, the information security professionals have asked me to specify what is meant by taking "appropriate technical measures" to ensure a level of security that is appropriate to the risk.

This has always been a very hard question for me to answer. I've seen myself as a data protection professional, not an information security professional. I've spent my working life reading data protection journals, not information security journals. Your organisation's information security lead should be accountable for defining what is meant by "appropriate," not you as the DPO. That person is (or should be) paid to know what the current state of the art is, what security standards are commonly expected in that sector, and what resources are required to ensure that these standards are being upheld. All you can do is advise on what the law provides and what your data protection supervisory authority expects. The GDPR provides that the following measures should be considered:

- the pseudonymisation and encryption of personal data;
- the ability to ensure the ongoing confidentiality, integrity, availability and resilience of processing systems and services;
- the ability to restore the availability and access to personal data in a timely manner in the event of a physical or technical incident; and
- a process for regularly testing, assessing and evaluating the effectiveness of technical and organisational measures for ensuring the security of the processing. [xcix]

It is your job to ensure that the information security lead individual has considered implementing these safeguards, but decisions about the extent to which your organisation implements any of these measures must be one that they are personally accountable for. DPOs should not be expected to determine what security controls must be in place. The GDPR only permits your organisation to appoint a DPO who fulfils *other tasks and duties* when they do not result in a conflict of interest.[c] In October 2016 the Bavarian data protection supervisory authority fined an organisation for appointing their Chief Information Security Officer as DPO,[ci] and in April 2020 the Belgian data protection supervisory authority fined a company €50,000 for appointing its head of compliance, audit and risk as DPO.[cii]

Is the DPO a team player or an umpire? The GDPR couches the role profile of a DPO in terms of being an umpire rather than a team player, and in most organisations a 'black or white' approach simply won't work. The GDPR expects DPOs to adopt a risk-based approach to their tasks.[ciii] Decent DPOs will know what degree of discretion is permitted and they will decide on the extent to which the available degree of discretion will be exercised.

For example, Subject Access Requests provide organisations with some latitude to determine whether and, if so, to what extent, to rely on an exemption in the SAR provisions to prevent the disclosure of some of the information that is processed about an individual. The DPO will be aware of what redactions could be applied and will probably determine whether the permitted redactions should be made – hopefully only after consulting the staff that are accountable for maintaining a good relationship with customers.

Displaying different leadership styles

What types of leadership styles do decent DPOs display? So much depends on the culture of the organisation and the resources that will be made available to you to meet your statutory obligations.[civ] I've known a few that operate as one-man-bands, working in virtual isolation from the rest of the organisation. I've known others who manage small and, in some cases, large teams. I've worked with privacy professionals who have failed because they have displayed a toxic mixture of leadership styles. I've also worked with privacy professionals who have failed because, when joining a new organisation or taking up the lead privacy role within their organisation, they had not adopted what was a winning combination in their previous role.

I'll use the list[cv] of leadership styles developed by the organisational psychologist Heather Bingham to explain what styles work well, and what styles work less well in the data protection field.

Autocratic

Does your organisation have a very hierarchical and deferential culture? Where job grade is seen as more important than actual technical knowledge? If so, as DPO you might feel it necessary to simplify quite complicated data protection concepts, perhaps using just a few PowerPoint slides, in order that more senior people but with little technical knowledge can skim read and formally approve whatever recommendations you will have drafted. An autocratic DPO may exist because virtually no one else in your organisation has sufficient knowledge – or interest – in data protection matters to challenge your recommendations. While competent DPOs may have the technical knowledge and experience to make quick decisions quickly, autocrats can also quickly feel overwhelmed with requests for advice and support. This hasn't prevented some from demanding to take all the decisions though, no matter how hard this will require them to them to work. Autocrats will find it hard to motivate the other members of their privacy teams if all the decisions are going to be taken by themselves. an. But autocrats don't care, as they usually have a strong narcissistic streak too. Avoid these people. It won't end well.

Charismatic

Great DPOs have vision and can influence and inspire others. This requires a mixture of technical skills and, frequently, a willingness to accept a relatively high privacy risk. What advice or action really is appropriate, given the circumstances? As I've mentioned in my letter on regulators, it is not always the best approach simply to reply on every piece of advice that is uttered by staff working for data protection supervisory authorities. Regulatory opinions are what they say they are – only opinions. Ultimately, only the courts can determine the true extent of privacy law. This approach requires DPOs to develop their own ethical approach to key issues of the day, and then sell this approach to their organisation. The late comedian Ken Dodd once remarked that he never took his audience for granted. For each performance he felt he needed to start afresh and woo them. The same approach is often adopted by charismatic DPOs.

Transformational

Some DPOs focus on outcomes. Teams must strive to work harder year after year. An ever-higher percentage of Subject Access Requests, for example, must be completed within the statutory time limits. Fewer data protection breaches must occur. Records of Processing Activities must be regularly audited. A greater proportion of staff must pass the organisation's annual privacy learning programme's knowledge test. Turnarounds for Privacy Impact Assessments must be improved. The daily grind of privacy work can be relentless, and while privacy metrics might improve, the morale of the staff at the privacy grindstone may not. If you're a transformational DPO then you should expect to deal with staff burnout. Don't run your privacy team too hot for too long. People will step back and rethink their lives. Life is too short.

Laissez-faire

An important way to promote accountability throughout an organisation is to educate and then devolve privacy decisions to others. This gives them an opportunity to better appreciate the data protection consequences of the decisions they take, particularly if they are then required to perhaps apologise personally to those who have suffered because of their misjudgements. I've found that this approach also gives individuals a greater sense of pride in their daily work and in the decisions they take. With effective supervision from the DPO, organisations can develop a strong culture of compliance that stands a good chance of being maintained when said DPO departs for pastures new.

Transactional

In my time, I've met few DPOs whose job profiles are supported by comprehensive operating instructions which explain precisely how each privacy task for which they are responsible should be completed. The absence of comprehensive sets of operating instructions can lead to inconsistencies of approach within privacy teams. When Data Protection Impact Assessments or Privacy Breach Assessments, for example, are carried out by different members of staff, perhaps working in different geographic locations, the lack of clear instructions explaining how to assess and weigh privacy risks can result in individual team members making very different sets of privacy recommendations to the organisation's project teams. Your team must offer your organisation a standard approach. Decent DPOs will ensure that comprehensive procedural manuals exist to safeguard against inconsistent approaches. This will enable your staff to feel more confident that they are doing the right thing as they carry out their privacy tasks.

Supportive

Decent DPOs find the time to coach their colleagues and direct reports, which is often the only way that they are eventually able to safely delegate some their privacy work to anyone else within the organisation. Nurturing these supportive relationships does take a considerable effort. It often takes time for the privacy message to sink in. Some elements of privacy law, including a good few of the technical requirements that are set out in the General Data Protection Regulation, are not easy to comprehend. DPOs many also find great value in engaging with the support networks that have created by organisations such as the Data Protection Forum, the National Association of Data Protection Officers and the International Association of Privacy Professional's KnowledgeNets. There is safety in numbers – or at least safety in appreciating that a DPO's approach to a particular privacy issue is very similar to that adopted by their professional colleagues. It's not just DPOs that will find value in engaging with these organisations – a decent DPO will encourage their direct reports to join them, too.

Democratic

Some DPOs prefer an inclusive approach, where all the key decisions are taken by committees. A weakness with this approach is that there is a risk that the key decisions may be delayed until all the issues have been considered by the committee members and they are unanimous in their view on the way forward. There is also a risk that other stakeholders, if their personalities are sufficiently strong, may override the reasoned assessments that DPOs make when forming their recommendations. Decent DPOs must always know when to accept that their advice will be ignored. But so long as this has been properly documented, and your advice had correctly interpreted the law, your organisation can't blame you should a data protection supervisory authority decide to take enforcement action for a privacy transgression that results from a failure to act in accordance with your advice. They may try, but the blame won't stick.

Decent DPOs will display a mixture of these styles. You lead a team and it's your job to inspire your team members. It requires effort: but this is what you are being paid for. Set an example. Do your best. Regrettably, I've also met a few privacy professionals who are just too tired to care too much about how they perform their day job. The demands placed upon them by their organisation, by virtue of the GDPR, have in some cases been overwhelming. Burnout definitely exists within the privacy profession. I say more about this in my letter on never giving up.

9 EDUCATION AND CONTINUING PROFESSIONAL DEVELOPMENT

Organisations that are likely to need to appoint a trained Data Protection Officer are:

- many public authorities;
- those where the core activities consist of processing operations which require regular and systematic monitoring of individuals on a large scale (e.g. CCTV); or
- those where the core activities consist of processing on a large scale of sensitive personal data (e.g. details of criminal convictions, health, racial origin).

In terms of your professional qualities, you are going to need much more than just a knowledge of data protection law. You need to have an "expert" knowledge of data protection law.[cvi] The GDPR doesn't specify the precise credentials you should have but whatever they are, they should provide you with a level of knowledge that is proportionate to the type of processing your organisation carries out, taking into consideration the level of protection the personal data requires. Where the processing of personal data is particularly complex or risky, your knowledge and abilities should be correspondingly advanced enough to provide effective oversight.

The Irish Data Protection Commissioner has advised that organisations should ensure that their DPO's qualifications and training is tailored to the context of the organisation's data processing:

The appropriate level of qualification and expert knowledge should be determined according to the personal data processing operations carried out, the complexity and scale of data processing, the sensitivity of the data processed and the protection required for the data being processed. For example, where a data processing activity is particularly complex, or where a large volume or sensitive data is involved (i.e. an internet or insurance company), the DPO may need a higher level of expertise and support. Relevant skills and expertise include:

- *expertise in national and European data protection laws and practices including an in-depth understanding of the GDPR;*
- *understanding of the processing operations carried out;*
- *understanding of information technologies and data security;*
- *knowledge of the business sector and the organisation; and*
- *ability to promote a data protection culture within the organisation.*

For example, a DPO may need an expert level of knowledge in certain specific IT functions, international data transfers, or familiarity with sector-specific data protection practices such as public sector data processing and data sharing, to adequately perform their duties. Taking into account the scale, complexity and sensitivity of their data processing operations, organisations should proactively decide on the qualifications and level of training required for their DPO. [cvii]

The General Data Protection Regulation isn't the only law you need to understand. Some of the other laws you should be aware of include:

- Data Protection Act 2018;
- Common law duty of confidentiality;

- Human Rights Act 1998 (especially Article 8 Privacy);
- Investigatory Powers Act 2016 (particularly if your organisation conducts covert investigations); and the
- Privacy and Electronic Communications (EC Directive) Regulations 2003 (if your organisation conducts direct marketing by any method other than post).

Don't worry too much if you don't yet fully understand data protection legislation. Hardly anyone does at the start of their career. Many of the 'legal experts' that profess to fully understand it don't have to implement it. They can lecture others on the law or get retained as a consultant to offer guidance on it (often for substantial fees), but they aren't usually spotted working for an organisation as a DPO.

Be careful how you use the knowledge that you will obtain. Don't set out to get bore or intimidate your colleagues with your knowledge of data protection technicalities too soon. As data protection consultant Tash Whittaker explained:

For all those starting out in data protection or looking to climb up the ladder, remember this; the best people I know in the data protection world, whose opinions I value the most, have never quoted an Article number or a Principle number at me. I know four Article numbers off the top of my head - 30, 6, 9 and 14 and that's only because other people say them all the time. If you are throwing Article numbers at people you are just doing the equivalent of name dropping. I'd rather talk about the content of the Articles and how they apply in real life than know the numbers. If you do throw numbers at me I will likely just look at you blankly. But if you ask me if you can do something and stay within the confines of the Regulation? Well, that depends... [cviii]

Before committing yourself or other members of your team to a data protection training programme, you should ask yourself several questions that will help identify what sort of programme is most appropriate: Do you just want you or your colleagues to be trained in the key aspects of the law? Do you want your colleagues to work with other staff who play a supporting role in the data protection function? What do you want your colleagues to do after the training? Do you want them to be accomplished all-round practitioners or just to be aware of the important detail that assists their job function? Do you want them to focus on specific issues (e.g. subject access requests or data transfers) or do you want them to know how to approach any data protection problem)?

Data protection qualifications & providers

Be wary of training providers that set their own syllabus, deliver the training, set their own exams and then mark them; this protects their own commercial interests in the syllabus and courses. You may well end up paying for paper qualifications that no one else respects. A wide range of accreditation options are available. Some training courses are one-day sessions, while some are online only. Others lead to academically accredited certificates such as diplomas from national law societies. There are also professional training programmes which are recognised internationally and offer professional qualifications that require an ongoing commitment to training to maintain the professional qualification.

The Irish Data Protection Commission recommends that organisation take the following factors into consideration when selecting the appropriate DPO training programme:

- *the content and means of the training and assessment;*
- *whether training leading to certification is required;*
- *the standing of the accrediting body; and*
- *whether the training and certification is recognised internationally.*[cix]

Data protection consultant Tim Turner has his own views on the qualifications that privacy professionals seek. Controversial as they are, they are worth bearing in mind:

I am a trainer. I've been teaching DP qualifications since 2008. I wrote and taught a certificated Data Protection course for three years. I have every incentive to tell you that qualifications are magic. They're not.

One training provider's qualification – made up of both basic and advanced components – involves just 8 hours of distance learning modules. That's the whole of data protection boiled down to just over a normal working day. A person cannot gain the GDPR's 'expertise in data protection law' in eight hours. It's bollocks.

If your DPO candidate touts a qualification, ask how long the course was, what it covered, and what the exam or test was like. The longer and more demanding it was, the more faith you can put in it. If the assessment was solely multiple-choice questions, forget it. Data protection is a complex subject that requires the ability to understand and communicate difficult ideas and choices. It cannot be reduced to 70-odd tick boxes.

There is no such thing as 'GDPR Certified'. GDPR Certification involves a processing activity being assessed and then approved by a certification body. That certification body needs official approval – in the UK, this will be delivered by the ICO or the UK Accreditation Service. GDPR does not provide for certification of people or products, and the UK has no privacy seals or kite marks process. Even GDPR certification – which won't apply to people – won't start until 2018 [sic] at the earliest. 'GDPR Certified' is a hoax.

Nobody offers a course free of issues. Courses run by the British Computer Society (BCS) offer an independent marking process. Competing training companies run the courses according to the BCS syllabus, but the exams marked independently. However, the exam itself requires rote learning and a phenomenal memory. A good DPO has the sense to consult the source text rather than relying on the Rain Man total recall that successful BCS candidates must possess. The International Board for IT Governance Qualifications (IBITGQ) also exists, but only accredits courses by one UK company (the same company that set the IBITGQ up and registered its website). Make of that what you will. The International Association of Privacy Professionals operate a popular and successful Certified

Information Privacy Professional qualification, but the content is not specific to the UK.

Many training companies run their own certificated courses (including one I wrote and delivered). Most have their merits; no course will turn a novice into an expert. Completing a course does not turn a person into a DPO – if it did, rather than paying consultants rates, why not pay for a member of staff to go on a course?[cx]

In the UK, there are several Data Protection qualifications on offer:

- two British Computer Society (BCS, formerly ISEB) qualifications (Practitioner and Foundation) delivered by BCS accredited trainers; [A Foundation Course is a course taken at basic level, preparing students for more advanced study. A Practitioner Course equips the delegate to works in the data protection profession.]
- two different Practitioner qualifications delivered and developed by two UK training companies;
- Foundation level qualifications from the International Association of Privacy Professionals (IAPP) (e.g. CIPP/E, CIPP/C, CIPP/E, CIPP/G, CIPP/US, CIPM, CIPT); and
- postgraduate qualifications (e.g. LLM) organised at many UK Universities.

According to data protection trainer Chris Pounder, who prepares candidate for the British Computer Society's (BCS) qualifications:

If you are choosing a Data Protection (DP) course for yourself or someone else, please first identify what you want the specialist training to achieve. Then consider the syllabus for relevant content, the level of training (e.g. Foundation, Practitioner), and the form of assessment as the demands made on the candidate by each type of course and assessment differ considerably.

If you are choosing a course for someone else, please discuss the items in the previous paragraph with that person. Employers should be prepared to support delegates with time off for revision/coursework if this is needed, especially for the BCS Practitioner qualification. If a delegate expresses a preference for a specific course, then this is likely to encourage them to do well in the assessment.

*Do not confuse **Foundation** level courses with the **Practitioner** level courses; in my view, the Foundation level is unlikely to equip Data Protection Officers from large organisations in all aspects of their role. BCS offer Foundation and Practitioner; Act Now and PDP offer a Practitioner course.*

Apart from BCS (which limits class size to 16 delegates maximum), class size information from other course providers is not published; this is important as it directly relates to the quality of delegate experience of the delivered training and some class sizes are large (and the profitability of the course for the training provider).

Only the IAPP and BCS qualifications approach ISO 17024 compliance; ISO 17024 sets out important attributes of any qualification scheme for staff (e.g. precise specification of the examined competencies; knowledge, skills and personal attributes obtained; independence of the examination and validity of the test of competence). (Actually, the IAPP certifications are the only credentials in the data protection field to be accredited under ISO 17024 - a globally recognised assessment framework for professional certifications.)

When choosing a course, seek the views of previous delegates (if you can).

There is a lack of transparency concerning independent oversight of all Data Protection qualifications; this is completely regrettable as it hinders consumer choice and the emergence of quality indicators for the training.

As a rule of thumb, the more complex or diverse the processing issues your organisation faces, the more depth you require from the training. It is well known that the UK's Information Commissioner uses the BCS syllabus to train his staff; however, not everyone may need this level of commitment.

The BCS Certificates (Foundation, Practitioner) are unique in that BCS does not deliver any training; it accredits training providers to deliver its data protection syllabi and sets and marks the examinations.

In other words, the BCS syllabus and examination process is completely independent from those who deliver the training. Training courseware is reviewed by BCS examiners on a regular basis and BCS can withdraw accreditation if training providers do not perform to the expected quality. Part of the Standard Operating Procedure is for BCS to sample the quality of training providers.

Sometimes training providers that are not certified to deliver a BCS DP syllabus, badge the qualification in their marketing brochures as their own, but sub-contract course delivery to a training provider that is certified. So you may need to identify who actually is delivering the training; this may be important to you if the training provider you are using is not certified to deliver the relevant BCS syllabus.

BCS & IAPP qualifications

If you need formal credentials to impress a prospective employer, data protection certifications are available from the British Computer Society or the International Association of Privacy Professionals. Certifications from other training providers are also available. The BCS offers a three-day Foundation Course which is intended to ensure that the team that supports the data protection function know the relevant details from the Act (e.g. PECR, data sharing, Human Resources, data protection principles, subject access, marketing). The course can be a staging post to the full six-day Practitioner Certificate. Candidates are required to answer a series of multiple-choice questions and write short essays. Those who are awarded the qualification will be able to demonstrate a good knowledge of legal definitions, the history and context of data protection; understanding the legal basis for processing personal data and the extra conditions for processing special category personal data; the obligations arising from each data protection principle, the options for transfers of personal data outside the European Economic Area; the rights of data subjects; how the data protection obligations apply to specific sectors such as marketing, CCTV, Human Resources and the Internet; Information Commissioners' notification and the full range of enforcement powers available to the Commissioner.

Alternatively, the IAPP offers a wide range of certifications to its members. Certifications include:

- CIPP/A (Certified Information Privacy Professional Asian Privacy, evidencing knowledge of the regional and international data privacy laws that govern data use in major Asian economies);

- CIPP/C (Certified Information Privacy Professional Canadian Privacy, evidencing knowledge of the federal laws such as the Privacy Act, PIPEDA and CASL, major provincial statutes, and emerging issues in Canadian privacy practice);

- CIPP/E (Certified Information Privacy Professional European Privacy, evidencing knowledge of Europe's framework of laws, regulations and policies, most significantly the General Data Protection Regulation);

- CIPP/US (Certified Information Privacy Professional US Private-Sector Privacy, evidencing knowledge of the interconnected webs of federal and state laws governing U.S. data privacy);

- CIPM (Certified Information Privacy Manager, evidencing knowledge of the skills to design, build and operate a comprehensive data privacy program); and

- CIPP/T (evidencing knowledge to include privacy in the design of technology products and services and to employ technical strategies to mitigate privacy risk.)

Students can take the IAPP courses in a variety of ways to suit them; online; through a virtual classroom on their computer screen that provides the same real-time back-and-forth of a physical classroom but without the traveling); or traditional, in-person learning. Students are examined by answering a series of multiple-choice questions. They are the qualifications to have go for if you don't feel it necessary to demonstrate much in-depth data protection knowledge.

How do you choose between the BCS and IAPP offerings?

According to Chris Pounder: *Apart from the IAPP and the BCS Foundation qualifications, all other data protection offerings are advertised at the Practitioner level. Do not equate **any** Practitioner courses with **any** Foundation level course.*

You should note that the IAPP's Foundation qualification focuses on regional national laws (Canada, USA, Asia and Europe). Its CIPP/E provides a foundational overview of the General Data Protection Regulation but it does not provide detail specific to the UK.

By contrast, the BCS Foundation is based on specific detail in UK law but it does not focus on the wider European dimensions, (although the course may be useful if the legislation is close to UK law such as the Channel Islands, Isle of Man or Eire).

Both Foundation courses need about 16 hours of training; this means that the BCS Foundation Certificate from will compete with "CIPP/E".

*The assessment for the CIPP syllabus is longer but at the end of the day, CIPP/E is a **foundation** level course. The IAPP website states: "When you* *earn a CIPP credential, it means you've gained a **foundational** understanding of both broad global and concepts of privacy and data protection law and practice plus you have knowledge of these components within your concentration.*"[cxi]

The BCS Foundation Course is ideal for categories of staff that have a job role connected with data protection (e.g. Data Protection contacts, IT specialists, Managers, SIROs and Information Asset Owners etc). It is also suitable for privacy practitioners working for organisations limited processing issues because its prime focus is Human Resources, data sharing, CCTV, subject access and electronic marketing. The Foundation Course can be seen as a staging post to the BCS Practitioner course as sometimes the Data Protection Officer cannot commit to the study time demanded by the Practitioner course.

The IAPP courses are mostly at the Foundation level. This may be surprising because individuals are encouraged by the IAPP to advertise their "CIPP/E" "(CIPP/US", "CIPP/C" designations as it promotes marketplace recognition of the IAPP brand. The IAPP has advised me that *"while we do use the phrase "foundational" with some of our programs, it is only to convey the strategic goal of providing a broad understanding of our field."*

The IAPP also offers "honorary" CIPP qualifications to a few leading data protection experts who are important IAPP sponsors or who are involved with IAPP in some way; whereas BCS for instance, require all trainers of its qualifications to sit the exam even if they have the Practitioner Certificate.

The IAPP also runs one of the very few courses approved by the French Data Protection Supervisory Authority, the CNIL, for purposes of certifying DPOs in France - the CDPO:FR designation is an amalgam of its CIPP/EU and CIPM designations.

Pounder considers that the BCS Practitioner exam is equivalent to a university undergraduate level. It can be challenging for those who have not experienced such written papers before, especially if their writing skills are rusty. Many employers fail to recognise that the BCS exam is a significant challenge and fail to appreciate that delegates often must use their own time to do the necessary revision. The BCS syllabus needs 40 hours of private study time.

Delegates who have obtained their CIPP Foundation qualifications can only maintain the use of their designation CIPP/E if they commit to Continued Professorial Education (CPE) and pay an annual certification maintenance fee. This means they have the cost of attending future IAPP events although non-IAPP events can count if approved by IAPP.

It's important to remember that an individual's IAPP certification lapses if their IAPP membership lapses.

There are many sponsors of the IAPP that pay large fees to the IAPP and these can be identified on its web- site. This payment, for instance, allows access of many staff to the IAPP Foundation certifications. It is this that gives rise to the "lock-in", as an individual who moves job to an employer who is not sponsoring the IAPP has to maintain an individual membership to maintain the right to use their IAPP qualifications.

Alternatively, if you don't wish to be bound by an obligation to continue to pay fees to the IAPP to maintain your qualifications, I recommend you seek a BCS qualification, even though it is a more difficult qualification to obtain.

Academic qualifications

At the start of my privacy career, few academics were interested in privacy and no universities offered academic degrees in data protection. Today, the academic landscape has exploded. According to Data Protection Trainer Chris Pounder: *the university qualifications are a different kind of training. For instance, the university qualifications are postgraduate, often research based, academically focused and spread over one or more years rather than one or two months. Assessment is usually continuous throughout the period of the course with a chunky dissertation at the end.*

If you are interested in a postgraduate qualification, the best known is probably the LLM offered at Northumbria University.[cxii] *However, you should also look at universities local to you (e.g. by contacting its Law or Information Management/Computer Science Departments). For instance, Dundee University has a M.Sc. in Records Management and Information Rights and other universities might have offerings around Human Rights and/or Information Law (e.g. Cambridge University Law Department, Queen Mary's University of London and the University of Nottingham).*

Clearly here, the more prestigious the university the more attractive is the course (and most likely the more expensive it is). Personally, I am very pleased that some of our BCS delegates have engaged with the subject so much so, that they have progressed to postgraduate studies on such university courses.[cxiii]

In the UK, students can study at Oxford University's Big Data Institute, an interdisciplinary research institute that focusses on the analysis of large, complex data sets for clinical research into the causes and consequences, prevention and treatment of disease. In the USA, in September 2020 the Georgia Institute of Technology announced the creation of a new School of Cybersecurity and Privacy, which is the first School dedicated to cybersecurity and privacy among major U.S. research universities. The institution had over 500 researchers in the field across and had won annual research contracts totalling over $180 million. Privacy research at the School was led by Peter Swire, a long-time participant at the annual CPDP conference. Along with its Ph.D. programme, the School offers three masters programmes, both online and off-line, including a Masters in Policy Studies.

Keeping pace with changes to data protection laws around the globe

For busy professionals in global teams, I really recommend bookmarking the free on-line legal summary provided by the legal firm DLAPiper. The firm publishes an excellent "Data Protection Laws of the World" website that contains valuable information enabling laws from over 100 countries to be compared and contrasted very quickly.[cxiv] Data protection comparison websites from other leading legal firms (e.g. Linklaters & Clifford Chance) are also freely available.

To keep up to date with privacy laws in Asia, Graham Greenleaf, a Professor of Law & Information Systems at UNSW Australia Faculty of Law and the Founding Co-Director and Senior Researcher of the Australasian Legal Information Institute, is an invaluable resource.[cxv] In 2021 Greenleaf was continuing his research on the global development of data privacy laws and agreements.

Data protection conferences & seminars

Try hard to attend some of the free conferences and seminars that the leading legal firms in London hold. You'll find a privacy event being held somewhere in the City of London most Tuesdays, Wednesdays and Thursdays. Attendances really drop off for events programmed on Monday mornings or late Friday afternoons. These events are useful exercises as they develop junior lawyers' presentation skills and offer key learnings to busy data protection professionals. As the UK lifts its COVID 19 restrictions in autumn 2021, an increasing number of these events are being held in person. They offer valuable networking opportunities and help reassure you that you are not alone. Maintaining a decent level of data protection knowledge is not easy. It is always reassuring to appreciate that other professionals also struggle to explain complicated privacy rules to their colleagues and develop policies that help their organisations comply with frequently changing legal requirements.

The more academically minded DPOs try to attend the Computers, Privacy and Data Protection conference, a three-day event devoted to privacy and data protection held in late January each year since 2007 in Brussels.[cxvi] Don't be disheartened by your first impression the conference venue – a tired exhibition hall (Les Halles de Schaerbeek) located in one of the more dilapidated parts of Brussels. The conference is split into two tracks. The first track is dedicated to experienced researchers (i.e. postdoctoral researchers, professors etc.), while the second track welcomes PhD students and junior researchers, lobbyists, consultants, civil society representatives, data protection authorities and European Commission officials. You should wrap up warm for the event – it's bitterly cold in Belgium at that time of the year. Don't be surprised if the event timetables slip as the event organisers are pretty lax with their timekeeping. Sessions tend to start later than advertised, the academic speakers take their time to get in their stride and you can expect them still to be speaking as the begowned clerks run through the rooms frantically ringing their handbells to signify the end of one session and the start of another.

In terms of timekeeping and content, the best run data protection conferences are organised by Stewart Dresner of Privacy Laws & business.[cxvii] He has a well-earned reputation for delivering events that start and end on time. The events are not cheap, but they offer good value for money for DPOs whose corporate expense accounts allow delegates to spend a few days at a renowned Cambridge University college in early July each year. The conference speakers, often including senior regulators and data protection policy specialists from the European Commission, accept invitations on the understanding that they will savour the university's world-famous ambience while simultaneously singing for their supper.

A very different conference experience is offered to the delegates that attend events run by the US-based International Association of Privacy professionals. These are large scale events, originally held on dates that did not compete with annual conferences run by smaller organisations, but the IAPP events are becoming much more frequent and are threatening the long-term future of their competitors. Ironically, European privacy practitioners support a US-based organisation that expands and threatens the commercial future of its European-based competitors. Whoever would have thought it. However, the IAPP conferences are the events that privacy pros like to be seen at, and where exhibitors pay decent money to showcase their latest privacy tech. Excellent networking opportunities are available to those that don't mind crowded spaces. Privacy celebrities are aplenty as the IAPP tries hard to create entertaining events. In March 2018 Monica Lewinsky an American activist, television personality, fashion designer and former White House intern delivered a keynote presentation on cyberbullying. I don't know whether many delegates attended the event to sympathise with her plight or just to gawk.

Much smaller-scale (and cheaper) events are hosted by the London-based Data Protection Forum and the National Association of Data Protection Officers. Despite the very low cost, the standard of the speakers and their presentations is often excellent. Here, delegates can mingle more freely with their peers. The data protection community is a notoriously indiscreet community. People tend to speak more openly in when they are in smaller groups. Keep your ears open and mingle. You are likely to learn something to your advantage.

Data protection newsletters, blogs and tweets

When you have any spare time, it's always worth checking to see who is writing, blogging or tweeting about what. I used to enjoy blogging and tweeting as @dataprotector, but I don't have the motivation to be as prolific as I once was. In addition to subscribing to the IAPP's daily dashboard[cxviii] for a summary of the latest data protection developments around the world, decent DPOs follow these commentators for a great insight on emerging matters:

- Jon Baines, a senior data protection specialist at Mishcon de Reya LLP curates the **informationrightsandwrongs** blog at https://informationrightsandwrongs.com/about/
- UK Information Commissioner John Edwards tweets as @JCE_PC
- Timothy Pitt-Payne QC, Anya Proops QC, Robin Hopkins and Christopher Knight, specialist barristers from 11KBW curate the **Panopticon** blog at https://panopticonblog.com
- Data Protection trainer Chris Pounder curates the **Hawktalk** blog at https://amberhawk.typepad.com/amberhawk/
- Data protection lawyer **Eduardo Ustaran** tweets as @EUstaran
- Data protection consultant **Pat Walshe** tweets as @PrivacyMatters

10 CAREER DEVELOPMENT

You can make a good living from a data protection career. You'll need to utilise your soft negotiating and influencing skills when negotiating your salary but don't give your organisation any expectation that they will be hiring an expert on all data protection laws around the world, as there are too many of them and the laws are changing too rapidly. Start by developing an expert knowledge of the UK's data protection laws. When you're confident with these, then you can look abroad. The ever-increasing sophistication of the world's data protection laws will require your organisation to seek specialist advice from experts that focus their knowledge in narrow subject areas. This advice is unlikely to be cheap: professional firms invest lot of money training their staff to deal with the issues that you will be presenting them with, and their fees will reflect the threat of a heavy regulatory fine in the event that your organisation fails to comply with the law.

I've already explained in my letter on education and continuing professional development that the organisations that are likely[cxix] to need to appoint a Data Protection Officer are:

- many public authorities;

- those where the core activities consist of processing operations which require regular and systematic monitoring of data subjects on a large scale (e.g. behavioural advertising, CCTV); or
- those where the core activities consist of processing on a large scale of sensitive personal data (e.g. details of criminal convictions, health, racial origin).

While the definition of a public authority[cxx] is clear, there has been confusion over the meaning of the term *core activities*. These are the primary business activities of your organisation. If your organisation needs to process personal data to achieve its key objectives, this is a core activity. This is different to processing personal data for other secondary purposes, which may be something your organisation does all the time (e.g. payroll or Human Resources information), but which is not part of carrying out its primary objectives.

There has also been confusion over the meaning of the term *regular and systematic monitoring of data subjects on a large scale*. This wasn't a term that was defined in the GDPR, but the European Data Protection Board considers[cxxi] that it includes all forms of tracking and profiling, both online and offline. If your organisation processes personal data for behavioural advertising purposes, it will need to appoint a DPO.

As far as determining if processing is on *a large scale* is concerned, I've previously explained in my letter on accepting risks that data protection supervisory authorities expect organisations to take several factors into consideration when determining whether the monitoring is sufficiently *large scale* to trigger the obligation to appoint a DPO. These factors are:

- the numbers of data subjects concerned;
- the volume of personal data being processed;
- the range of different data items being processed;

- the geographical extent of the activity; and
- the duration or permanence of the processing activity.

I've also previously explained that the Estonian Data Protection Inspectorate had suggested[cxxii] that data processing is of *large scale* when it includes:

- Special categories of personal data or personal data relating to criminal offences of 5000+ people;
- Personal data of high risk of 10 000+ people; or
- Other personal data of 50 000+ people.

Decent DPOs should ignore the European Data Protection Board's advice and apply my simpler test – which is that organisations should appoint a DPO whenever they monitor at least 10,000 people.

I've also already explained in my letter on regulators that just as DPOs were comfortably settling into their GDPR-mandated posts, in September 2021 the UK Government embarked on a consultation exercise[cxxiii] which queried the need for so many DPOs. While DPOs are required to report to the highest level of management, this doesn't mean the DPO has to be line managed at this level. However, they must have direct access to give advice to senior managers who are making decisions about personal data processing. Not surprisingly, the ICO supported the concept of the DPO:

We emphasise the significant skills and experience and professionalism that DPOs can bring. The DPO role under GDPR has also enabled more effective provision of independent advice within organisations and visibility in corporate governance at board level. It is important that those benefits are not lost as a result of any changes. It is also important that Government considers the potential economic impact of removing the requirement for DPOs as part of its overall assessment of the costs and benefits. This is because it is now a well-developed and skilled profession.

We also note that the requirement to appoint a dedicated role to ensure importance compliance functions are carried out is a widely used approach across many different sectors. It provides both assurance and expertise. For example, the FCA requires authorised firms and consumer credit firms to appoint an "approved person" to carry out "controlled functions". These include compliance oversight, money laundering reporting functions and senior management functions. The approved person must know and meet the FCA's regulatory requirements and understand how the FCA apply them.

Other examples include Schedule 46 of the Finance Act 2009 which indicates that, in "qualifying companies", a senior accounting officer must be appointed. Their role is to monitor the accounting arrangements of the company, and to identify any ways in which those arrangements are not appropriate tax accounting arrangements. The UK's Money Laundering Regulations 2017 require all businesses within the regulated financial services sector and some law firms to appoint a Money Laundering Reporting Officer (MLRO). The MLRO provide oversight for their firm's anti-money laundering (AML) systems, and act as a focal point for related inquiries. And employers who have five or more employees must appoint a competent person or people to help them meet health and safety legal duties as set out in Regulation 7 of The Management of Health and Safety at Work Regulations 1999. This competent person should have the skills, knowledge and experience to be able to recognise hazards in the business and help to put sensible controls in place to protect workers and others from harm.

We would encourage Government to consider how to retain the value, expertise and assurance that DPOs currently provide. This is particularly important in organisations with the highest levels of data use and consequently the highest potential risk to people. Having a dedicated role with responsibility for ensuring people's data is properly protected is an important safeguard. [cxxiv]

While the consultation exercise will end after I've written these letters, I would be surprised if too many organisations saw this as a golden opportunity to get rid of their DPOs. There is a risk that roles might be regraded if there was no longer a requirement for the DPO to report to the highest management level, so be prepared for a change in your reporting line.

Once appointed, your statutory tasks[cxxv] are:

- to inform and advise your organisation and your organisation's employees about its obligations to comply with the GDPR and other data protection laws;
- to monitor compliance with the GDPR and other data protection laws, and with your organisation's data protection polices, including managing internal data protection activities; raising awareness of data protection issues, training staff and conducting internal audits;
- to advise on, and to monitor, Data Protection Impact Assessments;
- to cooperate with the supervisory authority; and
- to be the first point of contact for supervisory authorities and for individuals whose data is processed (employees, customers etc).

In addition to monitoring the progress of their organisation's privacy programme, decent DPOs will prioritise and focus on the riskier activities, say where special category data is being processed, or where the potential impact on individuals could be damaging. Remember, DPOs provide risk-based advice to their organisations. If your organisation decides not to follow your advice, it should document the reasons to help demonstrate accountability.

What are you likely to read when you first come across a job advert which explains that an organisation is looking someone who is passionate about data protection? Expect to read a job advert which explains:

This role is responsible for providing the advice and oversight to ensure that we are fulfilling our regulatory requirements. You will fulfil all the responsibilities of a Data Protection Officer as defined in UK data protection law.

The role will require you to act as an advisor to Executive leaders, projects, and stakeholders on all data privacy regulatory matters. This will include the reporting to and advising the Executive Committee, Board, and regulators on a regular basis on our performance against our legal requirements.

You will also be accountable for delivery, facilitation, or influence of day-to-day operational activities to adhere with our Risk Management Framework. You will own the relationship with the UK data protection regulator, the Information Commissioner's Office including managing and reporting data breaches.

Other key accountabilities include owning and managing compliance with our transparency obligations including privacy notices, policies and customer-facing scripting, and owning the relationship with the parent company, in the context of data protection and privacy, ensuring synergies whilst acknowledging our status as a separate and independent data controller.

We'd love our Data Protection Officer to have these skills and experience:

- *strong communication and stakeholder management skills — for both internal and external relationships;*
- *leadership — both in terms of people and thought leadership;*
- *extensive data privacy experience within a similar organisation that evidences your ability to act as a DPO for an organisation with over 5 million customers and 7000 employees;*
- *very structured and well organised;*
- *experience of working closely with senior executives and*
- *display accountable behaviours and values — things happen because of you.*

We know it takes more than just skills and experience. So, we want our Data Protection Officer to:

- *drive, shape and further develop the data privacy culture across the organisation;*

- *lead and oversee our ongoing data privacy consultation (guiding the business on privacy related legal and regulatory risks and compliance options) ensuring the implementation of appropriate, lawful, customer friendly and commercially viable bases for processing personal data;*
- *build, lead, and coach a specialist team of data privacy experts to guide, advise and support the business in data privacy activities such as DPIAs, personal data incident management and third-party supplier due diligence;*
- *be a strong and effective leader and partner senior leaders across the organisation, influence and be credible; and*
- *work in partnership with wider assurance and oversight teams to ensure our data privacy Risk and Control estate is in alignment with both internal risk management framework and industry best practice.*

For this, you should expect to be paid a decent salary. The highest compensation levels can be found in the financial services sector. A decent DPO in the financial services field can expect to earn at least as much as, if not more than, the most senior staff at the ICO.

Don't accept a job where your role profile requires you to carry out tasks that may result in a conflict of interest with your role as DPO. I've already explained in my letter on teamwork that the General Data Protection Regulation only permits your organisation to appoint a DPO who fulfils *other tasks and duties* that do not result in a conflict of interest.[cxxvi] In October 2016 the Bavarian data protection supervisory authority fined an organisation for appointing their Chief Information Security Officer as DPO,[cxxvii] and in April 2020 the Belgian data protection supervisory authority fined a company €50,000 for appointing its head of compliance, audit and risk as DPO.[cxxviii]

You can, of course, be appointed as a DPO for a number of organisations at the same time. But don't take on too much. If you are appointed the DPO for a group of companies or public authorities, the data protection supervisory authority will still expect you to perform your tasks effectively, considering the structure and size of those organisations. Can you realistically cover a large or complex collection of organisations? You'll need to ensure you have been provided with the necessary resources to carry out your role, supported with a team if this is appropriate.

As DPO, you must be easily accessible and you should expect that your contact details are readily available to your employees, to the ICO, and the people whose personal data your organisation processes. Generic contact email addresses, i.e. dataprotection@[your organisation.com] are acceptable – and for security reasons are preferable to addresses that enable members of the public to readily know your real name. However, remember your organisation does have to provide your name when reporting a personal data breach to the ICO and to those individuals affected by it.

At some stage in your career, you may find yourself working for an organisation that has more than one DPO. While the General Data Protection Regulation provides that organisations must appoint a single DPO to carry out the statutory tasks I've already described in this letter, they can appoint other data protection specialists as part of a team to help support the DPO. If your organisation hires data protection specialists other than a DPO, it's important that they are not referred to as your organisation's Data Protection Officer, which is a specific role with requirements set by the GDPR.

As your organisation's DPO, you should expect:

- to be involved, closely and in a timely manner, in all data protection matters;
- to report to the highest management level of your organisation, i.e. board level;
- to operate independently and not be dismissed or penalised for performing your tasks;

- to be provided with adequate resources (sufficient time, financial, infrastructure, and, where appropriate, staff) to enable you to meet your statutory obligations, and to maintain your expert level of knowledge;
- to be given the appropriate access to your organisation's personal data and processing activities;
- to be given appropriate access to other services within your organisation so that they can receive essential support, input or information;
- to provide advice when your organisation carries out a Data Protection Impact Assessment; and
- to record your personal details as part of your records of processing activities.

All of this responsibility entails a lot of work. But what's the point of work? Journalist Elle Hunt pondered this question in an article published in The Guardian in October 2020, reporting how Anthropologist James Suzman had spent some 15 years based among the Ju/'hoansi Bushmen of eastern Namibia, who were notable for having sustained a foraging society well into the 20th century:

While he lived among them, he witnessed first-hand how the hunter-gatherer life was far from the constant struggle for survival many of us imagine it to have been. In 1966, a landmark anthropology paper had found that the Ju/'hoansi were generally well nourished and lived long, content lives. They used the bulk of their time to rest or have fun. Astonishingly, they spent just 15 hours a week finding food, and they stored little for the future, trusting in the surrounding desert to provide when required. Any individual surpluses were redistributed among the group. With social sanctions for selfishness and self-importance, their economy functioned in such a way as to eradicate inequality and material desires. Anthropologists concluded that the Ju/'hoansi worked almost exclusively to meet their immediate needs, beyond which their wants were few.

By contrast, in the corporate world – the world we know, where we might work 80-hour weeks largely untethered from any question of what is required and what is lusted after – our desires seem limitless, driven by an ever-escalating demand for growth and productivity.

In a 2015 YouGov survey, 37% of Britons said their work did not meaningfully contribute to the world. In 2017, a Gallup poll of 155 counties found that only one in 10 western Europeans described themselves as engaged by their jobs. This has been framed as a workplace issue – actually, says Suzman, "it is a problem with the nature of work". It reflects the 20th century boom in what the late anthropologist David Graeber dubbed "bullshit jobs", creating work for work's sake. From "Human Relations" departments that exist to improve attitudes to work and with-it productivity, to pay and bonus structures to further favour top earners, Suzman says there has emerged "a whole class of people who were utterly invested in this idea that they were actually creating value". The key to corporate success is convincing everyone else you're important and worthwhile, as Suzman learned for himself at De Beers.

"You developed vast bureaucracies which were ultimately pointless, but that was the skill: the bigger your bureaucracy, the more power you wielded and the more important you became. I established this vast empire – I don't think it made a jot of difference to anything when I got out."

For a self-identifying worker, it was an important reminder: if work is a transaction of energy, our own is finite.

As Suzman is talking, I consider work as the source of both my greatest satisfactions and my most miserable lows. I'd continue to do my job, and maybe even to periodically burn out, even if I had no material need to do so. My relationship to work may be the most significant in my life – but I am often made uncomfortably aware that the feeling isn't mutual.

For me, I tell Suzman – as I have told successive therapists, and with no small sadness – the hollowness emerges from a system that makes it seem both joyless and endless.[cxxix]

I don't think that all data protection work is both joyless and endless. But, as the ICO has constantly tried to improve data protection standards since the coming into force of the UK's first Data Protection Act in 1984, the compliance burden that DPOs are required to manage has become a real challenge. However, the exposure to the senior management team that the role brings can certainly help you move to another, equally senior role within your organisation.

Head-hunter David Wee explains what it takes to get promoted within large organisations:

You need to perform every day. But doing your job well will not necessarily get you promoted to big roles. Why? Only your manager knows you are good.

You need exposure with influential leaders. And if they have a positive image of you, they can help you get bigger roles.

In short, promotions are driven by three drivers- **Performance, Image and Exposure**.

Which of these have the greatest impact on careers?

Performance *contributes only 10% to your career growth. I was shocked when I first saw this finding. Early in your career, your ability to perform would contribute the most to grow your career quickly (90%). Why? Performance differentiates you from the crowd.*

Image and exposure. *As you progress in your career the importance of image (30%) and exposure (60%) takes on far greater weight. Why? Who knows your work best? Your boss, colleagues, possibly your bosses' boss. So if you do outstanding work, only a tiny slice of your organisation will know the quality of your performance. That's not enough if you want an accelerated career and a shot at the big roles.*

An example. We are in a succession planning session and your dream job is up for grabs. Your name is on the list. If no one knows you, no one (except your manager) will or can speak for you. In fact they may feel obliged to speak against putting an unknown into an important role. So although your performance might be superior you have little chance.

Is this fair? Of course not! Does it happen? You tell me!

So, make sure you are performing. But also take time to engage senior leaders and let them know how good you are, what you stand for and your contributions.[cxxx]

This advice neatly accords with Executive Coach Chuen Yeo's guidance:

Help your manager to succeed

Your manager hired you to perform a certain role and so if there are two people, one who makes his life hell and another a dream, who do you think he will put in good words when an opportunity arises? I'm not saying be a yes-man. You can be constructive and disagree without making it hell for people.

Seek out other sponsors

True story: I had a strong sponsor but because I only had one, I was passed over for promotion.

Beyond your own manager, go out and be visible. Build relationships with other departments and have them say good things about you to their bosses. When you are consistent your reputation precedes you. It'll then be easy for your name to be floated up for internal opportunities or even new portfolios.

Hone your skills and prepare yourself even when nothing seems to be happening

Be the undercurrent, I always say. Good things do take time to come your way and luck only goes to those who are prepared. Equip yourself with technical skills are present more future opportunities in your industry. Keep working on your soft skills because the higher you go, the more your job performance is based on how you make people feel.[cxxxi]

The three most important things I recommend that decent DPOs do early in their career is to network, network, and network. They should seek out others like them in the data protection field and keep in touch. Ask them about career opportunities and raise your own profile by getting involved in industry events. Conference organisers are constantly searching for new speakers. Get out there and get known. Most of the best data protection jobs are advertised by word of mouth, so keep your ear to the ground and start listening.

The recruitment industry is increasing concerned at the lack of sufficiently talented data protection professionals, and the difficulty in filling appointments in large organisations. However awful it is, there is a strong market for compliance professionals, so decent DPOs should ensure that all members of their data protection teams are also appropriately compensated to prevent too much staff turnover. Digital recruitment executive Fraser Merrifield gloomily reported in October 2021:

I just lost a candidate this morning to a £15,000 counteroffer.

What I'm not surprised about is bot the fact they had all this money in the bank to keep them – but the fact the candidate stayed, as it was only matching what they had elsewhere as a starting salary.

As with anyone I work with, I genuinely hope it works out well for them and that it turns out to be the best decision they have ever made – regardless I've helped them achieve a £15.000 pay rise overnight.

The employer even told them they would continue to counteroffer above this level to stop them leaving, therefor admitting they are worth even more to them than the counteroffer! But seriously, if you have employees that are worth £15,000 more than you are paying them, pay them what they are worth. Not when they decide to leave you for a better opportunity, but now!

Counteroffers are only accepted maybe 1 out of 20 times because they are a desperate attempt to save skills – if you want to keep your staff look after them!

- *Train them and develop them*

- *Pay them what they are worth, not what you can get away with*
- *Employ others around them so that they can up-skill alongside*
- *Have regular reviews with them around their position and career*
- *Invest in them before they have to come with their begging bowl*
- *Challenge them*

My job can be so frustrating when I have to tell a client that I've lost them an absolutely perfect candidate for their business, but it's equally as frustrating when I see companies pull out golden handcuffs to make it impossible for their staff to leave for something better.

What's the message here? Value your staff and more importantly value their career. It's worth a hell of a lot more to you than a desperate last-minute counteroffer.[cxxxii]

11 TOXIC RELATIONSHIPS

It probably won't be long before you will find yourself engaging with people who are difficult to deal with. I'm sure you've dealt with difficult people before, and that you'll be able to apply many of the skills you've previously used. You should expect those causing you grief to be aggressive, demanding and unreasonable. They may be people simply trying to exercise their information rights; they may be your fellow colleagues at your workplace, or they may be regulators who are investigating your organisation and are asking difficult questions. They may be quite unpleasant from the outset, or they may act in an insidious manner, undermining your confidence in a gradual, subtle way. You may feel stressed and frustrated, unable to do what has been asked, and even abandoned by those who you feel ought to be there to support you.

It's been said that data protection is, for some, a gift that keeps on giving. People want more and more information from and about themselves and your organisation and your capacity for responding to these requests can swiftly become exhausted. As a DPO, your job is to drive your organisation's compliance programme. This means that you should sometimes act as the applicant's champion and endeavour to provide them with the information to which they are entitled.

Data protection supervisory authorities increasingly want to inspect evidence that an organisation has thought an issue through. If your organisation relies on legitimate interest as a legal basis for processing personal data for a particular purpose, the authority may ask to inspect a completed Legitimate Interest Assessment. If your organisation has decided to process personal data in an innovative way, the authority may ask to inspect a completed Data Protection Impact Assessment. If your organisation has decided to send personal data outside the European Economic Area, the authority may ask to inspect a completed Personal Data Transfer Impact Assessment. Authorities may also ask for evidence that the assessments have been regularly reviewed. Additionally, organisations are required to maintain at all times Records of Processing Activities, which must include information about the purposes of the processing; the categories of data and categories of data subjects to which the processing relates; the organisations with whom the data might be shared, including in any third countries; and (where possible) how long the data will be kept for and what security measures are in place to protect it. Monitoring this lot requires you to curate a considerable amount of documentation. It is your job to keep it all up to date.

How can all this stuff be managed? Data protection laws were drafted with little thought to the practical and cumulative pressures that many organisations would face when being required to produce evidence of compliance with all its obligations. The compliance costs, in terms of running data protection compliance programmes that reflect these obligations are huge. Organisations face a choice: (1) whether to invest significant resources and purchase privacy tech that can evidence compliance with the legal obligations, including the delivery of the information rights that individuals may claim (and within the statutory deadlines that have been imposed); or (2) given the likelihood that relatively few people will ever exercise their information rights; train staff to respond to relevant requests without using any of the many automated tools available.

Many organisations decide not to invest in privacy tech and hope that their failure to maintain appropriate records or their failure to respond to requests within the statutory timescales won't result in people complaining in numbers that are large enough to attract the attention of the data protection supervisory authorities. Some of the organisations I've previously worked for have adopted this approach, and a few of them have got away with it. There is always a risk that the data protection supervisory authority will detect that your organisation took a deliberate decision not to complete detailed Records of Processing Activities, Legitimate Interest Assessments, Data Protection Impact Assessments and Personal Data Transfer Impact Assessments. Decent DPOs will mitigate this risk by ensuring that their organisation's risk register records this risk and documents which accountable executive will own it. Try to make sure that person isn't you. It ought to be the executive who declined to allocate you sufficient resources to complete these tasks.

Toxic customers

Relationships with customers can quickly deteriorate when Subject Access Requests (SAR) are poorly managed. I've explained in my letter on regulators that SARs are commonly used by unhappy people as tools to cause an organisation unnecessary work. Requests could be made by employees or former employees who were unhappy with the outcome of a disciplinary or a redundancy hearing. They might request all the information your organisation holds about them, rather than just information that relates to their grievance. Or customers, unhappy with the way their (probably) legitimate complaint was being dealt with might use a request as a way of causing your organisation extra work or to encourage your organisation to increase a settlement offer in return for the request being dropped. It is not appropriate to use the right of subject access for the purpose of corporate extortion. But it happens.

There will also be times when applicants are unhappy with the information that has been made available to them following their SAR. Mostly, this will be because the applicant feels that your organisation is hiding information from them. This may well be the case when your organisation takes advantage of the range of statutory exemptions that limit rights of subject access. In these circumstances, your organisation will need to explain to the requester that they have been provided them with the information they are entitled to access, rather than all the information the that was requested. I've occasionally been asked by a data protection supervisory authority to explain to the applicant what types of information has been redacted, and the reasons for the redaction. I have not usually explained what information has been withheld, nor why it has been withheld. While it may be good practice to be more open with an applicant, I have never found it necessary to be too transparent. The applicant may have wanted to know who their personal information was disclosed to, and what this information was. But if they are the subject of, say, a law enforcement investigation, providing the applicant with this information might result in you or someone else in your organisation, i.e. the discloser, committing a tipping off offence – for which you or they would be personally accountable for. I've tended to make good use of the exemption that allows organisations not to disclose information on the grounds that it may prejudice the prevention and detection of crime, the apprehension or prosecution of offenders or the assessment or the collection of a tax or duty or imposition of a similar nature.[cxxxiii]

On other occasions, the paucity of the response to a SAR might lead to the applicant to suspect that information was being unlawfully withheld and they would not accept that the reason for the thin response was because your organisation no longer held the information that had been requested. There have been times when I've responded to an enquiry from the ICO to explain that yes, my organisation did have a retention policy for a particular type of data and yes, on this occasion the information that had been requested had already been deleted in line with the retention standards that were set out in the policy. Decent DPOs will appreciate that their organisation can't be expected to reconstitute deleted data simply because someone asks for it.

Relationships with these requesters frequently turned toxic when they saw me as an agent of an organisation conspiring to deprive them of their rights. This was never actually the case. I never saw myself as a conspirator, working with others to deny someone what was due to them. A common problem was that too large an amount of information needed to be filtered to determine what material properly fell within the scope of a SAR. I once advised the DPO of an academic institution in Oxford who, following receipt of a SAR, had to inspect a huge cache of staff emails. The applicant, a senior academic, was determined to unearth material that cast him in an unflattering light. He wanted to know which fellow members of staff had expressed what he considered to be derogatory opinions about him. The email correspondence, written by fellow academics using university equipment in university time and at university expense, was damming, although from the context of the emails it was also clear that none of them had taken any steps they could later seek to rely on to argue that they were expressing confidential opinions. It was challenging to disclose information to the applicant without revealing the identity of other individuals. The decision on what to disclose involved balancing the applicant's right of access against their colleagues' rights relating to their own personal data. In the end, the applicant was permitted to read what his colleagues had written about him, but he wasn't permitted to know who said what.

In most cases where a duty of confidence does exist, it is usually reasonable to withhold third-party information unless you have the third party's consent to disclose it. In that case, I did what I could, assuming that the applicant was unlikely to want to remain in his post after he had learnt what the others thought of him.

During my time with a large mobile phone company, relationships with customers might turn toxic. This was sometimes the case when they applied for their mobile phone call records, which communication service providers are obliged to retain for 12 months. The police – and customers' solicitors – routinely accessed these records to pursue or defend investigations. The providers saw it as their social obligation to assist all applicants equally, so "Notes for Solicitors' were published, explaining the retention periods for all types of mobile phone records, what the records implied, and what procedures the applicants should follow to access them. Adherence to these procedures ensured that the records would be admissible when used in legal proceedings. Applicants could quickly become quite angry when they were told that the providers no longer held the information that had been requested. Many applicants were surprised that providers kept no records of the content of text messages that were sent and received. Others were upset that the call data records of each call recorded the links between mobile phones and the phone mast that received the strongest phone signal, not the links between mobile phones and the phone mast that was nearest to the phone.

Decent DPOs will moderate customer expectations and publish documents which explain in plain language what records are held, what the records mean, and just as importantly, what records are not retained.

My general approach with unhappy requestors is to remain as polite as I can, in the knowledge that any future ICO investigation will result in me making the email correspondence trails with the applicant available to the ICO - which would show that I was not acting in an unprofessional manner, and it was the requester who was making unreasonable demands. For this strategy to succeed, decent DPOs will need to adduce evidence that:

- the individual clearly has no intention to exercise their right of access. For example an individual makes a request, but then offers to withdraw it in return for some form of benefit from the organisation; or

- the request is malicious in intent and is being used to harass an organisation with no real purpose other than to cause disruption. For example, the individual:

  - explicitly states, in the request itself or in other communications, that they intend to cause disruption;

  - makes unsubstantiated accusations against you or specific employees which are clearly prompted by malice;

  - targets a particular employee against whom they have some personal grudge; or

  - systematically sends different requests to you as part of a campaign, e.g. once a week, with the intention of causing disruption.[cxxxiv]

Toxic colleagues

Relationships with your colleagues at work can turn toxic when you explain that you are not the only person in the organisation who is accountable for maintaining high data protection standards. It's your role to explain what is required of all employees – and to explain to the senior management team what is required from them in terms of ensuring that they delegate responsibilities to nominated individuals.

Like journalist Meghan Denney, I've encountered people with a range of abrasive personalities.[cxxxv] Some make you feel bad about yourself in order to build themselves up. I've worked with people who've tried to make me feel guilty about my success in my field and feel bad for them because of their own experiences. Don't feed into their resentment. Try complimenting them about their own work or share a tough experience you've had that day to prove you're human, too. Most people will relax when they realise they can relate to you more readily than they thought.

I've also met control freaks who have steamrolled projects, offended their co-workers and ignored the team dynamics. Often, simply talking to them about the issue solves the problem. Sometimes people are unaware of their own behaviour, and they need someone to draw their attention to it. Decent DPOs are paid to have difficult conversations with work colleagues. You're not paid to win a popularity contest. You should speak up.

Other colleagues may tell you one thing, but they won't deliver. Someone may acknowledge your great idea, but then present it as their own in a meeting. This two-faced behaviour is tricky because these people can seem authentic whenever you have direct contact with them, but they will put you down in private. To stop this behaviour, try talking to them. Yes, have another difficult conversation. Even though it may feel uncomfortable, that first move goes a long way. Try by actively listening and by remaining calm—don't feed into the drama but instead take what they say with a pinch of salt. Sometimes, one-on-one sessions won't solve an ongoing issue. If their behaviour continues, you should address it with your manager or with your organisation's Human Resources team. They can potentially mediate a formal meeting for you both to address the root of the problem.

Possibly the most annoying type of colleague is the constant critic. Nothing's worse than unsolicited negative feedback. When it happens non-stop and gravitates toward the mundane, that's when it becomes a problem. These people can be disarmed by directly engaging with them too. Start with an "I" statement, sharing your feelings. Tell them that you're grateful for their advice, but would appreciate a different approach, preferably with some positivity and less nit-picking. Do they refuse to stop? Say thanks and accept their judgment openly—if you can't get bothered, they may just stop.

Occasionally, you'll encounter a colleague who is unwilling to answer your totally reasonable questions or even acknowledge your existence. Such negativity can be especially concerning if you are in a new role, feeling unsure and searching for people to connect with. These colleagues aren't that easy to disarm. Keep in mind that you don't know their story. Perhaps you have the job they had applied for, or you've filled the vacancy that belonged to a good friend. They might just be completely intimidated by you. Try to get to know them on their own terms. While work pressures may cause them to be defensive and territorial, time and communication can mellow them. Meet them for a coffee or offer to assist with a project they are working on, but don't go overboard. It may take longer than you think to convince them to break down the walls, and some people won't crack. Show them some empathy and you just might get lucky.

Ultimately, when there is little prospect of a reconciliation, you may need to invoke your organisation's disciplinary procedure to dispense with the employee. Reputable organisations follow the ACAS code.[cxxxvi] This is a significant procedure which takes a good deal of management time and involves:

- a letter to the impacted individual setting out the issue;
- a meeting to discuss the issue;
- a disciplinary decision; and
- a change to appeal the decision.

If employers don't follow the ACAS code and the impacted individual wins an employment tribunal case against them, they could get a larger pay-out. Compared with their Asian equivalents, UK employment laws are quite strong. Staff can't be dismissed without good reason. Organisations can't make UK employees redundant and then advertise for a replacement head as soon as they have left without falling foul of a constructive dismissal claim. It is much easier to dispense with the services of contracted staff rather than full-time employees. Staff in countries such as Singapore can be dismissed with very little notice – and for very little reason. Decent DPOs should do what they can to maintain constructive and cordial, if not friendly, working relationships with all parts of their organisation. When it becomes too much to manage, they should consider the advice I've set out in my letter on never giving up.

Toxic regulators

Are there such things as toxic relationships with regulators?

There are certainly people working in data protection supervisory authorities who you won't trust, but hopefully these will be few in number. You may think of them as toxic, or the relationship you have with them as toxic, but in the most part they're just public servants trying to do their job. Your difficulty is that, on occasion, won't like the job they're trying to do. Decent DPOs tend to look on the bright side of life. The ICO's Regulatory Action Strategy commits the organisation to adopting a positive and proactive approach to ensuring compliance by:

- helping and encouraging organisations to understand and meet their information rights obligations more easily; and
- responding proportionately to breaches of information rights law.

This 'carrot and stick' approach means that the ICO aims to adopt a targeted, risk- driven approach to regulatory action – "*not using our legal powers lightly or routinely, but taking a tough and purposeful approach on those occasions where that is necessary*"[xxxxvii] If they keep to the spirit of this strategy, decent DPOs can develop productive working relationships with those that work for the ICO.

For more than 30 years I have found the ICO's staff to be extremely helpful whenever I've consulted them. Their pragmatic no-nonsense approach to resolving issues is also very welcome. This compares with a more distant approach I've experienced in other countries. Some data protection supervisory authorities act in quite a formal manner and it can be very hard to develop a productive working relationship with them. A lot of this has to do with cultural differences.

For example, the relationship between organisations based in Hong Kong and the Office of the Hong Kong Privacy Commissioner is much more formal than the relationship the ICO nurtures with the organisations it oversees. I once needed to contact the Hong Kong Commissioner's Office to register a potential data protection breach. A lot of doxing had been going on. Amidst a background of considerable social unrest, it was alleged on a prominent social media site that a (named) member of staff had unlawfully disclosed customer information to a local police officer. Before my organisation could begin the investigation, it was required to send a number of corporate policies to the regulator to reassure officials that any employee misbehaviour could and would be appropriately dealt with. The regulator appeared to be more concerned that the organisation had appropriate policies in place than in investigating whether a data breach had actually occurred. Eventually, following a full investigation by my organisation, no evidence of any misbehaviour was found. In reputational terms, however, the damage was done. News of the result of the investigation attracted much less media coverage than did the original allegation.

I've seen the ICO expand enormously during my privacy career. In early days, the office was frequently criticised for not taking action against those that ignored privacy laws, and perhaps this criticism was justified. A colleague at Google once explained to me that the paucity of legal resources at the ICO meant that the office would take great care before considering enforcement action against a tech giant. The ICO's enforcement team was small, the largest companies could so easily out gun them and delay their investigations for months. Enforcement action against these monoliths progressed at a glacial pace.

In later years, in an environment where significant GDPR fines were possible, regulatory enforcement action against organisations has snowballed. The European Data Protection Board's website regularly reports on the latest fine.[cxxxviii] In the UK, the ICO has focused on organisations that ignore the direct marketing rules that have existed for almost 20 years. The right to object to direct marketing is one of the strongest data protection rights that individuals have. It's also one of the easier issues for the ICO to take enforcement action on. When enough complaints have been logged, it's easy for the ICO to establish that customers have been caused annoyance and distress because of awful marketing practices.

It is too early to consider what impact the increased fining powers that are now available to data protection supervisory authorities has had on the relationship between organisations they supervise and the authorities. Some DPOs have distanced themselves from the authorities as they are wary of making unguarded comments about the state of their own compliance. This is a shame but, given the adverse impact on an organisation's reputation if any formal enforcement action is publicised, it is understandable.

I've often worked with the ICO's staff to ensure they appreciate how difficult it is for organisations to meet legal requirements. For example in 2021 I worked closely with the ICO to explain how hard it was for the organisation I was working for, a mobile phone company, to meet its data breach reporting requirements. Communication service providers were required to notify the ICO of all personal data breaches, no matter how minor they were, within 24 hours of becoming aware of the incident. Follow-up reports were required if full details of the incident and how it was being remediated were not available at the time of reporting. Unexplained delays resulted in a risk of being fined £1,000 for each late report.

I tried hard to assure the ICO's enforcement team that my organisation was doing its best to respect the reporting requirements. Both sides were fully aware that, with a large customer base, several minor incidents would inevitably need to be reported each day. A member of staff would work late each evening to complete the daily report – and the daily follow up reports – which would be acknowledged by a member of the ICO's enforcement team sometime later. Each side knew this exercise was largely a waste of time that diverted members of the data protection team from addressing more serious privacy issues. Not all mobile phone companies were as diligent as mine in reporting each breach. But the ICO took little action to encourage the relevant companies to standardise their breach reporting approach. The solution to the issue was simple – to change the law to require communication service providers to observe the same breach reporting standard that all other organisations subject to the GDPR had, i.e. to report significant breaches within 72 hours of becoming aware of the incident. This farce continued for months. The more compliant phone companies reported large numbers of incidents each week, while other providers reported very few.

Did it matter that there were different breach reporting standards for mobile phone companies?

Yes, if an enterprising journalist were to make a Freedom of Information request to the ICO about the different volumes of breach reports from each communication service provider. Why should my organisation be criticised for following the rules and reporting significant numbers of minor incidents? Why should organisations that didn't follow the rules so dutifully be spared any vilification?

As a DPO you are honour bound to follow the rules, no matter what the reputational impact on your organisation. Decent DPOs need private assurances that they are taking appropriate risks, whilst regulators need to publicly reprimand the reckless. Try as hard as you can to develop a trusting relationship with a regulator – then hope for the best that your contacts aren't transferred to another team too soon.

Toxic litigants

Organisations that report large data breaches often brace themselves for the next phase in the breach reporting cycle, which is dealing with unhappy customers. When the breach has been reported to the ICO and the senior management team has been appropriately briefed, the focus moves to containing the incident and reassuring everyone that the organisation really does take the security of its customers' data seriously. Hot on the heels of the senior management team and the worried customers will come claims management companies, on a mission to enrol as many victims as they can. They promise that, for a percentage of the claim, decent compensation will be available soon. The smaller print of the claims management company's engagement letter will explain that the company will retain some 35% of any amount won.

All is not lost. The business model of these companies has been thrown into question following an important High Court judgement on data breach claims in July 2021. As a result of the judgement, it may be uneconomic for claims management companies to fund groups of litigants.

I'll explain why. Data breach claims (both individual and group) are commonly issued together with notices of funding indicating that the claimant has costs protection by way of After the Event ('ATE') insurance and will seek to recover the ATE premium from the Defendant. The ATE premium often matches or exceeds the damages claimed in the action. But, ATE premia are not generally recoverable in civil litigation. There is a carve-out for 'publication and privacy proceedings' ('PPPs'), where ATE premia are recoverable, but the definition of PPPs includes proceedings for 'misuse of private information', or 'breach of confidence involving publication to the general public', but not data protection claims.

If the premia are not recoverable, the business case to fund the claims becomes questionable.

The judgement in this case, Warren v DSG Ltd, concerned a low-value claim brought against Dixons Carphone ('DSG') in relation to a 2018 data breach, in which external cyber-attackers had penetrated DSG's systems. The claim was brought in misuse of private information, breach of confidence, breach of the Data Protection Act 1998, and negligence.

DSG argued for summary judgement that the causes of action should be struck out or summary dismissed because: (1) breach of confidence ("BoC") and misuse of private information ("MPI") require positive wrongful conduct on the part of the defendant, and do not encompass a data security duty; and (2) there is no duty of care in negligence in respect of conduct covered by the data protection legislation (*Smeaton v Equifax plc* [2013] 2 All E.R. 959). The application was granted by Mr Justice Saini, holding that:

"[T]he Claimant's claim is that the DSG failed in alleged duties to provide sufficient security for the Claimant's data. That is in essence the articulation of some form of data security duty. In my judgment, neither BoC nor MPI impose a data security duty on the holders of information (even if private or confidential). Both are concerned with prohibiting actions by the holder of information which are inconsistent with the obligation of confidence/privacy. Counsel for the Claimant submitted that applying the wrong of MPI on the present facts would be a "development of the law". In my judgment, such a development is precluded by an array of authority."[xxxix]

Regarding the misuse of private information claim, Mr Justice Salini also held that: *I accept that a 'misuse' may include unintentional use, but it still requires a 'use': that is, a positive action.*[cxl]

The decision provides welcome clarity on the causes of action that can properly be brought in 'external attacker' data breach cases. Some legal commentators considered that it was of potential wider significance, given the inter-relationship of these causes of action and costs recovery: *As a result of this judgment, there must be (as a minimum) considerable doubt as to whether claimants can seek to recover ATE premia from defendants in 'external attacker' data breach cases and, if they cannot, as to the economic value of such cases for claimants.*[cxli]

Potential litigants were dealt a further blow in November 2021 when the Supreme Court announced its decision in the case of Lloyd v Google.[cxlii] It rejected a claim that sought billions of pounds in damages from Google over alleged illegal tracking of millions of iPhones. The decision was a significant victory for Google over the firms and funders of data protection mass claims. The Court held that the claimant had failed to prove that damage had been caused to individuals by the data collection but did not rule out the possibility of future mass-action lawsuits if damages could be calculated.

The reasoning of the court is straight forward: the right to claim compensation under the UK data protection framework can only be exercised by proving material damage or distress to each individual concerned, as that is what the law says and intended, commented data protection lawyer Eduardo Ustaran. *This is not necessarily the end of collective privacy actions, but those affected will be asked to evidence the damage or distress suffered.*[cxliii]

The case has been summarised by barrister Rupert Paines, who acted for one of the parties:

Between August 2011 and February 2012, Google is alleged to have installed software on Apple iPhones (described as the 'Safari Workaround'). The Safari Workaround allegedly had the effect of bypassing protections in Apple's Safari browser, setting a third-party marketing cookie on those devices whenever the user visited a website which contained DoubleClick Ad content. The DoubleClick Ad Cookie enabled Google to track those users across websites, and to harvest considerable amounts of information about their Internet usage and advertisement viewing habits. That, in turn, allegedly facilitated Google's distribution of targeted advertising to those users, for Google's ultimate profit.

Claims were brought against Google by individuals once this was discovered, both in the UK and US. Those were settled. Much more recently, however, Mr Lloyd (backed by very significant litigation funding) issued a representative claim for damages for breach of the Data Protection Act 1998, on behalf of himself and all those allegedly affected by the Safari Workaround (the "Class"). A representative action is a procedure of very long standing, by which a claim can be brought by or against persons as representatives of others who have "the same interest" in the claim. Mr Lloyd argued that that requirement was satisfied, since all the Class could claim damages for 'loss of autonomy' or 'loss of control' over their data, in a uniform amount, without the need for individual assessment of damages. The Class was estimated to number more than 4 million; the damages (though not quantified) running into the billions.

Mr Lloyd required permission to serve the claim form outside the jurisdiction, as Google is based in the US. Google resisted the permission application on the basis that the conditions for a representative action were not established: in particular, because the class had (ex hypothesi) differing entitlements to damages, and 'loss of control' damages were unavailable in English law.

Mr Lloyd lost in the High Court; succeeded in the Court of Appeal; and lost in the Supreme Court.

The decision led to calls for the Government to step in to make it easier for groups of consumers to take action over data breaches.

Jim Killock, Executive Director of the Open Rights Group, agreed:
There must be a way for people to seek redress against massive data breaches.[cxliv]

How the Government will respond, though, is unclear.

12 INTERNATIONAL ISSUES

I've worked for organisations that have had offices in most parts of the world and have been impressed with the very different attitudes that employees and customers have about their privacy. My experience is that few people in the developing world express much of an interest in data protection or privacy matters. Perhaps this will change. However, very few individuals outside the EU have ever contacted firms I have worked for and exercised any of the information rights that local data protection laws prescribe. Even fewer employees have ever exercised their information rights either. I assume that this because of differences in local employment laws and local employment cultures which promote a much greater degree of deference to their superiors in the management chain.

Harmonising European data protection laws

In my letter on education I explained that the legal firm DLAPiper publishes an excellent Data "Protection Laws of the World" website that enables DPOs to look up the key features of the privacy and data protection laws in more than 100 countries.[cxlv] Free resources such as these are invaluable. Data protection comparison websites from other leading legal firms (e.g. Linklaters & Clifford Chance) are also freely available.

I won't spend much time explaining how data protection laws have developed across Europe, but it is always helpful to know where to find a quick summary. If you are really interested in knowing what laws were passed, why and when, you can do no better than refer to the guide entitled "European Data Protection Laws & Freedom of Expression," published by the University of Cambridge's Centre for Intellectual Property & Information Law.ᶜˣˡᵛⁱ The guide describes the key developments in three chronological periods: 1973-1994, 1995-2016, 2016-2021.

First Generation (1973-1994) – Data Protection Convention

During this period, data protection at pan-European level reflected the provisions of the Council of Europe's Convention for the Protection of Individuals with regard to Automatic Processing of Personal Data (ETS 108), which was adopted on 28 January 1981 and entered into force for those a party to it on 1 October 1985. The adoption of data protection legislation at State level began with the Swedish Data Protection Act 1983. In total, eighteen States currently within the European Economic Area (an organisation comprising the member states of the European Union plus Iceland, Liechtenstein and Norway) as well as Switzerland and the UK adopted data protection legislation during this period.

The Convention's provisions were reflected in UK law through the coming into force of the Data Protection Act 1984.

Second-Generation (1995-2015) – Data Protection Directive

During this period the European Union became the dominant pan-European actor within the data protection space because of the adoption of Directive 95/46/EC on the Protection of Individuals with regard to the Processing of Personal Data and on the Free

Movement of such Data on 25 October 1995 (following an initial proposal going back to 27 July 1990). The Directive required action by EU States by 24 October 1999 and was also adopted by the wider EEA with a date for implementation of 26 June 1999. All EEA States (the EU states plus Iceland, Liechtenstein and Norway) were required to enact data protection legislation according to a common template. The directive continued in effect until 25 May 2018.

The Directive's provisions were reflected in UK law through the coming into force of the Data Protection Act 1998.

Third-Generation (2016 - 2021) – General Data Protection Regulation

This period began with the coming into force of EU Regulation 2016/679 on the Protection of Natural Persons with regard to the Processing of Personal Data and on the Free Movement of such Data and Repealing Directive 95/46/EC on 25 May 2018 across the EU, alongside a specialised Directive which applied in the area of law enforcement (Directive EU 2016/680). The General Data Protection Regulation is in principle directly applicable in law throughout the EU Member States although approximately one third of its provisions require State-level implementation and leave considerable discretion to individual nations. The GDPR was adopted by the wider EEA and entered into force on 20 July 2018. Directive 2016/680 was not adopted by the EEA.

The GDPR's provisions were reflected in UK law through the coming into force of the Data Protection Act 2018.

The UK has now entered a new phase, which can be described as:

Fourth-Generation (2022 onwards) – UK Data Protection Divergence

This period began with the publication in September 2021 of a Government consultation paper[cxlvii] setting out a series of wide-ranging proposals to rethink some of the key data protection rules.

The consultation paper contained a number of proposals which included:

- a relaxation of several areas of the GDPR, with a focus on outcomes rather than prescribed processes;
- plans to increase enforcement powers under the UK's Privacy and Electronic Communications Regulations (PECR) to match those under the GDPR, sending a clear warning to those flagrantly disregarding marketing rules by sending nuisance calls and text messages; and
- plans to change the governance structure of the ICO, bringing its operations more in line with those of other regulators such as the Competition and Markets Authority, Financial Conduct Authority and Ofcom.

The Government's stated aim was to drive economic growth and innovation and strengthen public trust in use of data in the UK. This would be achieved by alleviating some of the more prescriptive GDPR obligations on organisations, whilst retaining a robust data protection regime built largely on existing laws. The Government hoped that any changes would be broadly compatible with EU equivalency, enabling the UK to continue to exchange personal data with the EU as it currently does. I've discussed the potential impact of these proposals in my letter on regulators.

Transborder data flows

Data protection supervisory authorities are very keen to ensure that personal data is appropriately protected when it is sent to other countries. Accordingly, many countries have data protection laws that restrict transfers of personal data outside that country unless the rights of the individuals in respect of their personal data are protected. It was reported in August 2021 that in China, changes to the Personal Information Protection Law will require cross border transfers to be protected by standard contract clauses that will be developed by the Cyberspace Administration of China. [cxlviii] It is not clear how closely these clauses will align with the EU's model clauses. Regrettably, the rules on what restrictions are placed on transfers of personal data, and when an exemption applies, aren't at all easy to follow.

Sending personal data sent outside the EEA

Decent DPOs need to know that a transfer of personal data outside the host country is known as a 'restricted transfer.'

The most common tool that organisations based in the EU use when making a restricted transfer to an organisation in country outside the EEA is to ensure that the sender (the 'data exporter') and the recipient (the 'data importer') have entered a contract which contains the standard data protection clauses that have been adopted by the European Commission. These are known as the 'standard contractual clauses', SCCs or the 'EU model clauses').

The clauses contain contractual obligations on the data exporter and the data importer and provide rights for the individuals whose personal data is transferred. Individuals can directly enforce their rights against the data importer and the data exporter. The European Commission updated the clauses in June 2021 to reflect the GDPR's provisions and the decision by the European Court of Justice in the Schrems II case[cxlix] which, in July 2020, had struck down the EU-US Privacy Shield agreement.

The Schrems II decision followed litigation between the Irish Data Protection Commissioner and Facebook Ireland Ltd & Maximillian Schrems. The Court found that "essential equivalence" with EU law also applies to the model clauses. It confirmed that these standards must be based on EU law, particularly the EU Charter of Fundamental Rights, and not on Member State law. The Court confirmed that EU data protection supervisory authorities must suspend or prohibit data transfers if the model clauses cannot be complied with or if protection of the data cannot be otherwise ensured. The decision put pressure on the authorities to suspend data flows from the EU to the USA under the under the Privacy Shield agreement, which had provided an alternative tool for the transatlantic flow of data between the two regions. The court cited concerns with US surveillance law, which it interpreted as unacceptably degrading European data subjects' rights under the GDPR when that data entered US borders as the main reason for striking down the agreement.

Organisations were given a very short period, which spanned the 2021 summer holiday season, to prepare for and to use the new model clauses. The old model clauses were formally repealed on 27 Sept 2021.

Some DPOs welcomed the updated causes because they are designed to be more flexible than the previous sets. They include a docking provision that makes it possible for companies to join and exit group arrangements for data transfers, although it was not initially clear how easy it would be to use the provision, particularly when different organisations used different types of security controls to protect personal data.

Other DPOs reacted with anger and incredulity on reading the new clauses and the accompanying guidance that had been prepared by the European Commission. They were concerned that the burdens imposed on their organisations, particularly on small businesses, that needed to use the model clauses were enormous. The new procedures added new layers of complexity to what was already a tedious process. To meet the requirements of the Schrems II decision, for example, for each data transfer, organisations acting as data exporters must verify on a case-by-case basis whether the law or practice of the third-country importer may compromise the effectiveness of the SCCs. When the data exporter determines the law or practice of the third country is not deemed *essentially equivalent* to that of the EU, organisations must implement supplemental measures, such as those recommended by the European Data Protection Board, to raise protections to the level required.[cl]

But how can that be achieved? The European Data Protection Board recommended that organisations carry out a complicated six-step process to ensure that each transfer complied with the new rules:

- map the data transfer, including onward transfers to sub-processors of personal data to third countries;
- verify the tool the data transfer relies on. If there is an adequacy decision, monitor that it remains in place;
- assess whether, in the context of the transfer under consideration, anything in the law and/or practices of the third country may have a negative impact on the effectiveness of the SCCs;
- identify and adopt the supplemental measures needed to bring the level of protection of the data transferred to the standard of EU essential equivalence;
- take any practical steps that adoption of supplementary measures may require; and
- at appropriate intervals, re-evaluate the level of protection afforded to the personal data transferred to third countries and monitor any changes in circumstances that may affect it.

Even organisations with mature privacy programmes and deep resources to devote to data protection compliance found these new obligations extremely onerous and burdensome. The work that needs to be done can't solely be carried out by your organisation's privacy team. Project managers are required to co-ordinate and track the progress of multiple data processing agreements that are being negotiated simultaneously. Complying with these obligations also requires engagement with the data users, who ought to know what personal data they have and where it is processed; the records management team, who need to keep your organisation's data maps constantly up to date; the procurement team and the legal team; and the external audit team, who play a vital role in assuring that the exporter's representations are valid. The cumulative impact of the risk analysis, documentation and monitoring requirements on any organisation is substantial.

The new SCCs were introduced at a time when many organisations were still reeling from the GDPR requirement to maintain up to date data maps of their own data flows. The new obligations also place onerous requirements on your organisation to ensure that all your suppliers have comprehensively documented how they process the personal data that is passed to them. Your legal team will find tools like the SCC Generator[cli] helpful to select the appropriate text from the SCCs, but you should not underestimate the compliance burden on your organisation.

If you are the DPO for a small or a medium-sized organisation, you will not have and you almost certainly won't be able to afford the external legal support and other staff to carry out all the tasks that are recommended in the European Data Protection Board. The burden is so significant that many organisations run the risk of a data protection supervisory authority asking, considering their non-adherence to the recommendations, whether they should be transferring any personal data to suppliers that are based outside the European Economic Area at all.

What action the supervisory authorities will take in the light of widespread non-adherence to the European Data Protection Board's recommendations is not clear. Given their lack of enforcement of the cookie rules for so many years after the ePrivacy rules came into force, it is possible that many supervisory authorities will decide that an organisation's failure to act in accordance with the Schrems II decision is not an issue that has an especially high regulatory enforcement priority. But, given the reservations that some of the German Länder (state) data protection supervisory authorities have expressed about data flows to the USA, it is reasonable to assume that some of these authorities - and in particular the Baden Wittenberg Baden-Württemberg Authority - are not interested in helping the organisations they supervise address the challenges raised by the Schrems II decision.[clii] They simply don't want the personal data of German citizens to be exported to the USA.

The ratchet further tightened on German companies in June 2021 when some of the state data protection authorities formed a task force to assess, by means of questionnaires, the extent to which the companies had reacted to the *Schrems II* decision. There were real concerns that the authorities would use the information gathered through the questionnaires to initiate enforcement proceedings should a company not be able to document a sufficiently high level of compliance.[cliii]

If the purpose of the Schrems II decision was to nudge EU-based organisations into taking decisions about supplier contracts that will result in personal data remaining within the EEA, then its success will depend to some extent on whether EEA-based suppliers can offer contractual safeguards and commercial terms that are as compelling as those offered by their non-EEA competitors. It is often much cheaper to outsource functions to organisations in India and Asia because employment costs within the EEA are generally much higher than those in the developing world. But is it right that a fortress Europe should impose significant and, in my view, frequently unnecessary regulatory burdens on organisations that wish to export data (and therefore jobs) from the EEA? That's a question that is best answered by DPOs that work inside fortress Europe.

The reality is that personal data is likely to continue to flow to organisations around the world, and the European Data Protection

Board's recommendations will be ignored more often than they are adopted.

Sending personal data outside the UK

Having left the EU in January 2020, the UK was no longer required to replicate the transborder data flow rules that had been developed by the European Commission and the European Data Protection Board. In August 2021 the ICO consulted on a new tool, the International Data Transfer Agreement ("IDTA"), which it hoped would be of more practical use for organisations that exported personal data from the UK.[cliv]

For the accompanying draft guidance, the consultation asked questions around the transfer of personal data and on broader issues such as when a relevant transfer is deemed to have taken place. In one interpretation of the rules, the return of personal data by a UK-based processor to an overseas controller would not be considered a restricted transfer. Does a transfer of personal data to an entity already directly subject to the UK GDPR constitute a restricted transfer? The ICO indicated that it did not intend to rely on this approach.

The consultation also asked whether exporters should be required to attempt a transfer mechanism before relying on the derogations, and whether the requirements for the derogations to be *necessary* should be interpreted as *strictly necessary*.

The ICO's draft Transfer Risk Assessment ("TRA") tool was designed to assist organisations when making routine transfers. The tool involved a three-stage process for assessing risk. The consultation invited feedback on the draft IDTA, including whether it was sufficiently clear how the IDTA should be used in conjunction with the TRA tool, whether organisations were likely to use it, whether a modular approach (such as that taken by the European Commission in its new SCCs) would be preferable, and whether the ICO should provide a separate multi-party IDTA.

The three-stage TRA process is:

First, organisations should establish that the tool is suitable for its transfer (e.g., the transfer is routine rather than high risk). As part of this assessment organisations must consider several factors, such as the nature of the importer, any onward transfers, the purpose and method of transfer, and its regularity.

Second, organisations must assess whether the IDTA would be enforceable in the destination country. If there was doubt, organisations should carry out a supplementary risk assessment to assess the potential for harm to data subjects and identify extra protections that may reduce the risk. The consultation provided guidance as to when the risk of harm would be assessed as low, moderate or high, for example deeming basic employment or contact information to be low risk. The consultation also provided guidance as to factors that may reduce or increase the risk of harm to data subjects, with automated decision-making by the importer constituting one risk factor, as well as guidance on measures that may be implemented to supplement the IDTA.

The final step was to assess the destination country's regime for regulating third-party access to personal data, including an assessment of surveillance laws. Again, the consultation provided guidance as to factors that were likely to safeguard the rights of data subjects and factors that were likely to undermine them, as well as guidance on assessing the likelihood of third-party access. The draft tool specified that the transfer should only go ahead where the destination's regime was sufficiently similar to the UK's, the risk of third-party access was minimal, or the risk of harm to data subjects was low even in the event of third-party access. Specifically, the TRA tool stated: *If you decide… the risk of harm to data subjects is low even if there is concerning third party access, you may proceed with the restricted transfer using the IDTA together with the extra steps and protections you identify.*[clv]

The draft template IDTA did not follow the same structure as the EU model clauses. Instead, it provided separate sections for details of the parties, the transfer (including whether the importer is permitted to make further transfers and the frequency with which the IDTA will be reviewed), the data transferred and the purpose of the transfer, as well as the security measures that will be implemented at each stage of the transfer. The IDTA also included "Mandatory Clauses" which set out the exporter's and importer's obligations with respect to the transfer. The Mandatory Clauses included provisions regarding how the exporter and importer would ensure that appropriate safeguards were in place with respect to the transfer, compliance with ICO requests, the actions to be taken in the event of a personal data breach, onward transfers and sub-processing and data subject rights.

The ICO also proposed publishing additional guidance templates, covering, for example, optional TRA extra protection clauses, commercial clauses, and examples of a completed TRA and IDTA.

Finally, the consultation invited comments on whether the ICO should issue an IDTA in the form of an addendum to existing model transfer agreements, such as the EU model clauses, and provided a template Addendum that amended the EU model clauses to work in the context of UK data transfers. The Addendum would potentially provide a practical compliance solution for many companies transferring personal data from the EU and the UK, which would otherwise be required to put in place separate data transfer agreements.

Decent DPOs will await the outcome of this consultation exercise with anxious anticipation. It will necessitate a mammoth repapering exercise that will deliver relatively few benefits to individuals - unless you're lucky enough to be a data protection lawyer that specialises in amending data protection contracts.

The influence of the Court of Justice of the European Union

Decent DPOs will be mindful of the Court of Justice of the European Union's influence on interpreting European data protection laws. The Future of Privacy Forum's EU Policy Fellow Sebastiao Barros Vale has explained that:

According to the EU Treaties, EU Member-States' courts may – or, in case no appeal from their decisions is possible, must – ask the CJEU to rule on the interpretation and validity of disputed provisions of EU law. Such decisions are known as preliminary rulings, by which the CJEU expresses its ultimate authority to interpret EU law and which are binding for all national courts in the EU when they apply those specific provisions in individual cases.

Since May 2018 – when the GDPR became applicable across the EU -, the CJEU has played an important role in clarifying the meaning and scope of some of its key concepts. For instance, the Court notably ruled that two parties as different as a website owner that has embedded a Facebook plugin and Facebook may be qualified as joint controllers by taking converging decisions (Fashion ID case), that consent for online data processing is not validly expressed through pre-ticked boxes (Planet49 case) and that the European Commission Decision to grant adequacy to the EU-US Privacy Shield framework is invalid as a mechanism for international data transfers, and supplemental measures may be necessary to lawfully transfer data outside of the EU on the basis of Commission-vetted model clauses (in the Schrems II case).

Ever since the enactment of the 1995 EU Data Protection Directive, the CJEU had a prominent role in expanding the scope of protection afforded to individuals by data protection law, in a way that ultimately influenced the text of the GDPR. Some notable examples include landmark rulings on the definition of personal data (in the Breyer and Nowak cases), the lawfulness of transferring data to countries outside of the EU (in Schrems I) and the so-called "right to be forgotten" (in the Google Spain case).[clvi]

There was, as of November 2021, a long list of questions that the court had been asked to clarify next. Notwithstanding the departure of the UK from the European Union. Decent DPOs will be keen to monitor the CJEU's decisions and track the extent to which the ICO decides to adopt them. Barros Vale has listed the key questions that concern:

- clarifying essential aspects of personal data protection;
- accountability and due diligence;
- administrative enforcement; and
- judicial redress.

Clarifying essential aspects of personal data protection: right of access; lawful grounds for processing data for targeted advertising

Both the very active Austrian Supreme Court of Justice and the Austrian Federal Administrative Court have sent questions to the CJEU about the information that controllers are required to hand over in response to data subjects' access requests.

In March 2021, the former asked the EU's highest court, in a case involving the Austrian Postal Office, whether under their right of access data subjects must be informed about the categories of recipients of their personal data even in the cases where specific recipients have not yet been determined, but disclosures to those recipients are planned for the future. Or should they only be informed about the categories of recipients with whom personal data was already shared?

More recently, in August 2021, the Federal Administrative Court sought clarifications from the CJEU regarding what obtaining a "copy of the personal

210

data undergoing processing" means. In this respect, the Court asks whether such a right entails receiving entire documents/database excerpts in which the personal data are included or a mere "faithful reproduction" of the personal data processed by the controller. If the latter is the case, the referring court also wishes to know if there are exceptions to the rule, for the benefit of data subjects' comprehension. Lastly, Austrian judges also query whether the information that should be made available to data subjects in a "commonly used electronic format" is only the "copy" of the personal data or also all the elements of Article 15(1) GDPR (e.g., information about the purposes of the processing and data retention periods).

Two very complex sets of questions in cases involving processing of data for targeted advertising purposes on social media have also reached the CJEU in 2021. The Court's answers are likely to shape the future of how social media companies and online advertising businesses process personal data in the EU.

The first one, from April, comes from the Higher Regional Court of Düsseldorf, Germany in a first case of its kind, combining antitrust and data protection enforcement. In a case involving Facebook, the Court asks the CJEU if data collection through user interfaces placed on third party websites or apps that relate to Article 9(1) GDPR protected attributes (e.g., political party or health-related outlets) counts as processing special categories of data. Should people that visit such websites or apps or use the company's plugins therein (e.g. "Like" buttons) be considered to have manifestly made their sensitive data public? As the European Data Protection Board (EDPB) has already provided guidance on these matters, it will be interesting to see to what extent the CJEU will endorse the EDPB's interpretation or diverge from it.

The Court also seeks to clarify whether personal data may be lawfully collected and combined by the company when obtained from other Facebook Group services and third-party websites/apps to offer personalised content and advertising, under the "contract" or "legitimate interests" legal bases. In parallel, the Court asks the CJEU to rule on whether GDPR-compliant consent may be effectively and freely expressed by users "to a dominant undertaking".

These last questions resemble others that were posed more recently by the Austrian court. On July 20, 2021, the Court essentially asked the CJEU … to clarify whether the social media platform can rely on "contract" as lawful ground for processing personal data for personalized advertising, or whether it should rely on consent of its users under the GDPR (by asking against which of these two lawful grounds should the wording of its terms and conditions be assessed).

In addition to the consequential question about the appropriate lawful ground in this particular context, the Austrian court also invited the CJEU to clarify how the data minimisation and purpose limitation principles as provided by the GDPR should apply in the context of personalised online advertising, in particular when it comes to sensitive data.

Accountability and due diligence

The German Federal Labour Court's reference of October 2020 invites the CJEU to shed light on the circumstances that may lawfully lead organisations to dismiss their appointed Data Protection Officers (DPOs). The EDPB DPO guidelines state that "a DPO could still be dismissed legitimately for reasons other than for performing his or her tasks as a DPO (for instance, in case of theft, physical, psychological or sexual harassment or similar gross misconduct)". With this reference, the German court seeks to understand whether the CJEU shares the same view and, if so, whether Article 38(3) GDPR would preclude a German provision that forbids employers from terminating the employment relationship with their DPOs in all cases, including for reasons other than the performance of the latter's tasks.

Additionally, the referring court asks the CJEU whether the GDPR limitations on dismissal also apply to those DPOs who are appointed pursuant to a domestic law obligation, where the GDPR itself does not require their appointment.

Looking at a different accountability-related obligation, in a June 2021 reference, the Bulgarian Supreme Administrative Court wishes to know if the mere occurrence of a data breach is sufficient to ascertain that the controller has not implemented appropriate technical and organisational measures to prevent the breach. In case of a negative answer, the CJEU is asked to further provide a benchmark against which national courts may assess the appropriateness of the implemented measures.

Administrative enforcement: How far can DPAs go and do antitrust authorities play a role?

In a set of questions from March 2021, the Budapest Regional Court aims to ascertain how far the GDPR-prescribed independence and corrective powers of Data Protection Authorities (DPAs) go. While it seems to be clear that individuals and companies have a right to lodge a judicial appeal against DPAs' decisions or their inaction (see Article 79 GDPR), the Hungarian court highlights situations where both DPAs and courts are simultaneously called by individuals to assess the lawfulness of the same data processing operations.

Should DPAs have priority competence to determine GDPR infringements? Or should both DPAs and Courts independently examine the existence of an infringement, possibly arriving at different conclusions? May a DPA find a GDPR breach where, in parallel proceedings, a court has found that there was no such breach? The CJEU is thus expected to clarify how the ne bis in idem principle manifests under the complex enforcement system of the GDPR.

In another case already mentioned above the Higher Regional Court of Düsseldorf seeks to clarify the fundamental question of how antitrust law enforcement and data protection rules interact and whether antitrust regulators may play a role in safeguarding data protection law as part of antitrust proceedings.

This case started from a 2019 decision of the German federal antitrust authority (against Facebook. The authority found a breach of German competition law with regard to abuse of market dominance by also relying on GDPR provisions in its assessment. These findings primarily concerned rules around valid consent for combining personal data across several services of the social media company. One of the measures imposed by the authority was a prohibition to collect user and device related data obtained from the use of its affiliated services, as well as from visits to third-party websites or apps without valid consent from users.

Facebook appealed the decision before German courts, with the court of appeal (Higher Regional Court of Düsseldorf) expressing doubts on the legality of the decision of the antitrust regulator, and deciding to suspend its effects as an interim measure until the matter is decided on substance. In return, the German Federal Court of Justice's antitrust division overturned this interim measure of the court of appeal, and decided that the prohibition ordered by the German federal antitrust authority can be enforced while judicial proceedings are ongoing, before sending the case back to Düsseldorf to be decided on substance.

The court in Düsseldorf suspended proceedings and asked the CJEU to clarify a number of essential questions (see also Section 1 above). In this context, can the German federal antitrust authority determine a GDPR breach by the company investigated in antitrust proceedings and order its correction, given that the regulator is not a supervisory authority under the Regulation, let alone the lead one? The referring Court noted that the Irish Data Protection Commissioner – as the lead DPA of the company – was already investigating alleged GDPR breaches relevant for this case.

Judicial redress: Can competitors engage in representative actions? And do "worries" and "fears" count as non-material damages?

An interesting question posed by the Austrian Supreme Court of Justice in December 2020 relates to whether persons other than harmed data subjects may initiate judicial proceedings for GDPR breaches against the infringer. The Austrian court wishes to know if Article 80(2) GDPR allows competitors, associations, entities and Chambers to sue, regardless of invoking specific data subjects' rights infringements and the latter's mandate, in cases where such bodies are entitled to initiate proceedings under national consumer law.

On such matters, the literature argues that Article 80(2) leaves it up to Member-States to determine whether non-profits with public interest statutory objectives and which are active in the defence of data subjects' rights may bring own-initiative proceedings in their territory. Thus, it will be particularly interesting to see how the CJEU views the ability of competitors to sue other companies in putative defence of data subjects' collective interests, notably in the absence of alleged infringements of individuals' rights.

In May 2021, the Austrian Supreme Court of Justice asked important questions to the CJEU related to non-material damages under the GDPR: can courts attribute compensation to data subjects where a GDPR provision has been infringed, but the data subjects have not suffered harm? And, if demonstrating harm is necessary, does Article 82 GDPR require data subjects' non-material damages to go beyond the mere nuisance or discomfort caused by the infringement?

Just a month later, the Bulgarian Supreme Administrative Court went further and asked whether data subjects' worries, fears and anxieties caused by a confidentiality breach involving personal data qualify as non-material damages which entitle them to compensation, even where data misuse by third parties has not been established and/or data subjects have not suffered any further harm.[clvii]

Decent DPOs needn't hold their breath waiting for the outcome of these cases. According to its 2020 Annual Report, the average length of proceedings at the CJEU was currently 15.4 months.[clviii] DPOs should wait even longer for decisions concerning the really complex issues, like the interaction between antitrust and data protection law.

13 OPEN-MINDEDNESS

In my letter on doing the right, I mentioned psychologist Oliver Burkeman's observation that often, by doing your thing – as opposed to what you think you ought to be doing – you kindle a fire that helps keep the rest of us warm.[clix]

Don't work on the basis that laws are inalterable and that they must always be applied to the issue you are currently dealing with. While most laws were passed to prevent or to regulate a known issue, they can't always be easily applied to new and emerging issues or technologies. If a law has unintended and perverse consequences, decent DPOs should take risk-based decisions on the extent to which the law should be ignored. As the renowned philosopher and statesman Edmund Burke noted in 1780: *Bad laws are the worst sort of tyranny. In such a country as this they are of all bad things the worst, worse by far than anywhere else; and they derive a particular malignity even from the wisdom and soundness of the rest of our institutions.*[clx]

Unfortunately, the parliamentary timetable doesn't always allow proper pre-legislative scrutiny. According to journalist Andrew Rawnsley:

Ministers ram through immense slabs of often badly thought through law with far too little invigilation. Individual MPs do not have the time or the expertise to scrutinise everything coming out of government, with the result that they will often end up voting for laws they do not understand, and might not agree with if they did, because they have been ordered to do so by their whips.[clxi]

There are many examples of badly thought through laws. Take the case of the UK Government's ill-fated initiative to legislate against dangerous dogs during the summer of 1991, when a series of media stories drew attention to children being attacked by these animals. Evidently, something had to be done – and quickly. Such was the (media induced) public concern that a Dangerous Dogs Act was rushed through Parliament, receiving Royal Assent on 25 July.[clxii] As was the custom at the time, relevant trade bodies were asked by the relevant Government Department (in this case, the Home Office) to carry out some pre-legislative scrutiny and make comments on the proposals. The Association of British Insurers, who I was working for at the time, and which had a particularly close relationship with the Home Office, was given a deadline of little more than 48 hours to respond. Given such a short period for reflection, the ABI had nothing of consequence to say. Within days, the Government's proposals had become law.

Amidst great publicity, the Act made four breeds of dog illegal to own, breed from, abandon or sell: the Pit Bull terrier, the Japanese Tosas, the Dogo Argentino and the Fila Braziliero. But no thought was given on how to determine whether a dog was one of those types. It's not something that even an experienced RSPCA officer can easily determine. Dogs that attracted the attention of the authorities weren't usually owned by the type of person that had complete documentary evidence establishing the animal's lineage. And its impact? Negligible. Dangerous dogs didn't disappear. A review five years after the implementation of the Act found no significant reduction in dog bites. Adult hospital admission rates for dog bites tripled in England between 1998-2018 while the incidence of dog bites in children had remained consistently high. According to vet Robin Hargreaves:

It is clear from current evidence that the Dangerous Dogs Act has not improved human safety around dogs. Furthermore, the focus on breed specific legislation has detracted from efforts to properly understand the motivation behind serious dog attacks - an understanding which might have allowed us to better educate dog owners and the public at large on how to have a healthy relationship with dogs that is both safe and fulfilling for us and free of unnecessary fear and anxiety for dogs.[clxiii]

The RSPCA reported that over a third of the people killed by dogs over the next five years were attacked by legal breeds.[clxiv]

Another example of a badly thought through law concerns the rules protecting online privacy. An early policy aim was to ensure that individuals were better informed about how information that related them or their electronic devices was used to improve their browsing experience, and how they could choose whether to receive direct marketing messages. However, there was little evidence that many individuals had the time or the inclination to become more aware of how their data was being processed. Nor was there much evidence that, unless prompted, many people would exercise the choices that they would be empowered to have.

The initial 2002 European ePrivacy Directive[clxv] provided that:

Member States shall ensure that the use of electronic communications networks to store information or to gain access to information stored in the terminal equipment of a subscriber or user is only allowed on condition that the subscriber or user concerned is provided with clear and comprehensive information in accordance with Directive 95/46/EC, inter alia about the purposes of the processing, and is offered the right to refuse such processing by the data controller. This shall not prevent any technical storage or access for the sole purpose of carrying out or facilitating the transmission of a communication over an electronic communications network, or as strictly necessary to provide an information society service explicitly requested by the subscriber or user.[clxvi]

In 2009 the Directive was amended to require consent for the storage or access to information stored on a subscriber or users' terminal equipment. In other words, it imposed a requirement to obtain consent for cookies and similar technologies. Member States were required to amend their local laws to facilitate this.[clxvii]

The Directive now provided in Article 5.3 that:

Member States shall ensure that the storing of information, or the gaining of access to information already stored, in the terminal equipment of a subscriber or user is only allowed on condition that the subscriber or user concerned has given his or her consent, having been provided with clear and comprehensive information, in accordance with Directive 95/46/EC, inter alia, about the purposes of the processing. This shall not prevent any technical storage or access for the sole purpose of carrying out the transmission of a communication over an electronic communications net work, or as strictly necessary for the provider of an information society service explicitly requested by the subscriber or user to provide the service.[clxviii]

European countries had until 25 May 2011 to make the relevant changes to their local laws.[clxix]

Much of this information, however, might not at the time have fallen within the scope of the definition of personal data, as the organisations using this data for marketing purposes didn't want to or need to know the identity of the individual browsing the internet. For their purposes, it was sufficient to know that a user of a particular electronic device was browsing websites that published a certain type of information, e.g. information about foreign holidays, new cars, or financial investments. Browser manufacturers intended to use this information to charge companies selling foreign holidays, new cars or financial investments a premium for sending marketing messages to users who, by virtue of their recent online behaviour, were more likely to be interested in that product or service.

For months, Data Protection Officers debated what individuals should know about what cookies and internet browsers did, and what choices the browser manufacturers should allow their customers to make. Some considered it unfair that individuals could only surf the internet on the condition that their on-line browsing behaviour was used to develop profiles for targeted marketing purposes. Individuals ought to be able to prevent their on-line activities from being known and used (and therefore monetised) by advertisers and other organisations they had never heard of. As the Regulation put it:

"Where required, measures may be adopted to ensure that terminal equipment is constructed in a way that is compatible with the right of users to protect and control the use of their personal data."[clxx]

The European Commission's view was that the solution was straightforward: before information was taken from an individual's device, the individual would need to consent. But how could organisations that did not interact with individuals obtain the user's consent? What about cookies that were set on user devices because they were necessary for a website to function? How many individuals were really bothered about the on-line tracking that was taking place? Some might have found it slightly irritating, but how many people really thought the practice utterly objectionable? On the Internet, anything can be objectionable to some people, but was the harm caused by online tracking so significant as to require action of the type the European Commission wanted?

What followed, in the UK at least, was a couple of years of discussions between the owners of Internet sites, browser manufacturers, Internet search engines and the ICO. There emerged a general agreement that cookies designed for targeted marketing purposes should be capable of being decommissioned by users if those users objected. Cookies designed for other purposes should not. It was also agreed that individuals could be considered as having consented to tracking cookies being set on their electronic devices if they had not changed their browser settings. This was welcome news for the browser industry. Consumers hardly ever touched their browser settings, so their on-line behaviour continued to be monitored (and monetised).

DPOs in some organisations subsequently tried extremely hard to implement the new rules, explaining what types existed to their customers. Clever explanations were devised by people who had no idea whether anyone was interested in reading them. Verisign explained to its users that:

There are three different types of cookies:

- *Session cookies: these are mainly used by online shops and allow you to keep items in your basket when shopping online. These cookies expire when the browser is closed.*
- *Permanent cookies: these remain in operation, even when you have closed the browser. They remember your login details and password so you don't have to type them in every time you use the site. The law concerning permanent cookies stipulates that they need to be deleted after a period of six months.*
- *Third-party cookies: these are installed by third parties with the aim of collecting certain information to carry out various research into behaviour, demographics etc.*[clxxi]

The top layer of a typical layered public sector cookie notice advised individuals that:

We have placed cookies on your device to help make this website better. You can use this tool to change your cookie settings. Otherwise, we'll assume you're OK to continue.[clxxii]

A second layer provided more information, such as:

Some of the cookies we use are essential for the site to work. We also use some non-essential cookies to collect information for making reports and to help us improve the site.

The cookies collect information in an anonymous form.

To control third party cookies, you can also adjust your browser settings. Users will then be presented with buttons either to turn cookies on or off, and to check a statement indicating that that they are happy with the choices they have made.[clxxiii]

At the bottom of the page, users were given a button to click OK to indicate that they wanted to continue to browse the Internet.

Compliance with the ePrivacy Directive was patchy at best, with organisations struggling to change their practices in line with the new rules. The coming into force of the GDPR, and the raising of the standard of what level of transparency was required before individuals could truly have been considered to have consented to cookies being placed on their devices, caused huge problems. In September 2021 the UK Government highlighted two key issues:

- *organisations' ability to collect audience measurement data in order to improve their websites and services for their customers had been affected by the stricter consent requirements that are intended to give consumers greater control over how their data is used; and*
- *individuals frequently complain about the number of cookie pop-ups on websites. The available evidence to suggested that many people do not engage with privacy information and controls, and simply accept the terms or use of cookies because they want to access the website. The use of nudge techniques may encourage users to provide consent or turn off privacy protections*[clxxiv]

The Government consulted on two main options for tackling these issues. The first option would permit organisations to use analytics cookies and similar technologies without the user's consent. In effect, these cookies would be treated in the same way as 'strictly necessary' cookies under the current legislation for which consent is not required. The second option could permit organisations to store information on, or collect information from, a user's device without their consent for other limited purposes. This could include processing that is necessary for the legitimate interests of the data controllers where the impact on the privacy of the individual is likely to be minimal - such as when detecting technical faults or enabling use of video or other enhanced functionality on websites. Decent DPOs will agree with the argument that users might reasonably expect a data controller to carry out such activities without their consent anyway. They will track the outcome of this consultation exercise with great interest.

Let's return to today's data protection world. Don't expect all data protection laws to be precise. Burke also remarked: *It is the nature of all greatness not to be exact.*[clxxv] Decent DPOs will use their own common sense to determine what feels right and will act on their own intuition.

Former Information Commissioner Elizabeth France characterised good data protection practices as *applied common sense*. Accordingly, decent DPOs will adopt a pragmatic and principled base approach to data protection compliance. If the strict interpretation of a legal requirement, in particular cases, had perverse consequences, it isn't necessary to adhere to that legal requirement. Your organisation should not expect a data protection supervisory authority to take enforcement action following a failure to do something which, if it had had acted as the law required, might well have resulted in individuals being caused inconvenience or, even worse, harm.

Data protection supervisory authorities need to be open-minded on these issues, too. It's not sufficient for them simply to expect organisations to ensure that their products or services meet the requirements of regulation. The authorities, together with Government officials, have an equally important responsibility to work with organisations not only to ensure that the obligations are understood but also to ensure that legal requirements are fit for purpose.

Much UK legislation is proposed as an afterthought, to apply a remedy when something has already gone wrong. The purpose of that piece of legislation is to prevent whatever went wrong from going wrong again. But what unintended consequences will flow from the new legislation? And will those unintended consequences help or hinder responsible organisations that strive to comply with data protection laws? Government officials try hard to draft laws that meet the political requirements of the moment, but they don't always work. Data protection trainer Chris Pounder's Hawktalk blog[clxxvi] frequently criticises officials from the Information Commissioner's Office & the Department of Digital, Culture, Media and Sport for their failure, as he sees it, to think matters through and to properly respect individuals' rights.

Anya Proops QC made the following observations on the Government's proposals to introduce an Online Safety Bill in August 2021:

The UK Government's recent introduction of an Online Safety Bill has raised afresh the important question of the extent to which online intermediaries can and should be required to curate and police the content that they host or index online. The Bill itself is controversial. Not least there are serious questions as to whether, as currently framed, it will: (a) require intermediaries to meet excessively burdensome standards (b) subject Ofcom (the proposed regulator in respect of the relevant online safety duties) to regulatory obligations which are themselves Augean in nature and further (c) fundamentally undermine the free speech rights which the Bill itself recognises are foundational to a modern digital democracy. In other words, there is a serious question as to whether this is a Bill that will do more harm than good.[clxxvii]

Decent DPOs don't take a Talmudic approach to data protection. Don't make extremely fine distinctions, concentrating on minute details and subtle hair-splitting. I've never wanted to force detailed and, in hindsight, often pointless changes on organisations. What is so wrong with so many organisations' current privacy practices? Naturally the practices should be designed to prevent individuals being caused significant harm or annoyance, but I've never seen the point in privacy micromanagement. This approach does not work in a society that has a legal system which is underpinned on common law principles. It probably works better in countries that rely on legal systems that embrace a more structured, codified approach, such as that which exists in mainland Europe, where specific rights and obligations are imposed on individuals and organisations. One where the recipients only have rights if the law specifically prescribes these rights.

I prefer the approach where individuals and organisations are permitted to take whatever action they chose unless a law has specifically restricted or prohibited that action.

As I write, there is currently a sense of unease within some parts of the data protection community about the extent to which the UK, having left the European Union, will develop standards that depart from the requirements of the GDPR. Some DPOs are concerned about the implications of 'the Brussels effect', a term which describes the power of the European market and the dependence of the UK on it. The imperative need for the UK to have continuing access to personal data from the EU will limit its scope to diverge from the GDPR. Some have argued that the UK cannot engage in data trade with the EU without having essentially equivalent data protection, which limits its control over its data protection laws.

According to Professor Paul Schwartz of the UC Berkeley School of Law, the UK is unlikely to diverge too far from GDPR standards: *The EU is a large commercial market, and the UK's IT sector, like the UK export sector in general, is highly dependent on data transfers from the EU. Moreover the EU has an impressive regulatory capacity for data protection, and one exercised by numerous institutions. As for the ability of the private sector to create different data-driven services for different markets, this issue proves highly contextual depending on a company's services, internal resources, and other factors. Some companies benchmark different aspects of their use of personal data throughout the world using the GDPR as their critical measure. Such global decisions may be driven by a combination of political, policy or ideological reasons, however, and not merely because the underlying services are non-divisible. None the less, it is probable that many global companies have found it beneficial to adhere to EU privacy standards rather than customise for different markets.*

As a related matter, and as noted above, the acceptance of EU data protection by companies like Apple, Google and Microsoft made it easier for the UK to remain with the bandwagon rather and try a new direction upon Brexit. The result was both a de facto and a de jure Brussels Effect. It was de facto because companies emulated EU regulations worldwide. As a result there would be some likelihood that these organisations would follow it post Brexit within the UK. The impact of this behaviour as well as other influences contributed towards a de jure Brussels Effect in which the UK adopted EU law domestically.

Another factor was that the existing law of the UK at the time of Brexit was the GDPR. At that point the transaction costs of exit from that legal framework would have been high, and, during Brexit, the UK chose to pick its battles. There is no other data privacy model as accessible as EU data protection, and the conceptual costs of starting from zero were – and are – daunting. Put differently, some exits within the overall Brexit were more important than others, and regarding data protection law, there was no desire in the UK to undertake change, especially considering the high costs of doing so.[clxxviii]

Some organisations are unlikely to grasp the opportunity to move away from the GDPR. Having altered their practices to meet GDPR requirements, the leading global tech companies will probably be unwilling to incur additional legal compliance costs to meet new British laws. Intelligence and law enforcement agencies in the EU are likely to be particularly keen to ensure the UK continues to have its data protection laws assessed as adequate by the EU in order that personal data can continue to flow for intelligence and law enforcement purposes.

However, now the UK has left the European Union, it is entitled, as incoming Information Commissioner John Edwards explained to Parliament's Digital Culture Media and Sport Committee in September 2021[clxxix], to adopt a Fleetwood Mac approach and to "go its own way" when developing appropriate data protection laws. Yes, we can go our own way. If I were a European data protection supervisory authority, I wouldn't expect the UK to accept without question all the European Data Protection Board's opinions. Beware the defiant Brits! Beware perfidious Albion!

There's nothing wrong with reviewing data protection issues through the lens of your own organisation's commercial interests. But it's also your job to ensure that your organisation treats personal data in ways that meet the ordinary expectations of individuals – including those that are sufficiently engaged in data protection issues to be very vocal in their concerns about how their personal data is being processed. But, just as organisations should pay attention to their customers' legitimate concerns, policymakers that set unrealistic data protection standards should also take care.

Beware of the mob – or at least the small and frequently unrepresentative group of privacy activists whose loud voices can cause much more anguish than their numbers would otherwise imply. As Rudyard Kipling explained in his poem 'The Weeds of Runnymede', which commemorated the signing of the Magna Charta in June 1215:

> *And still when mob or monarch lays*
>
> *Too rude a hand on English ways,*
>
> *The whisper wakes, the shudder plays,*
>
> *Across the reeds at Runnymede.*

And Thames that knows the mood of kings,

And crowds and priests and such like things,

Rolls deep and dreadful as he brings

Their warning down from Runnymede! [clxxx]

But decent DPOs should trust their instincts, and they'll be fine.

14 NEVER GIVE UP?

I explained in my letter on doing the right thing that psychologist Oliver Burkeman recommends[clxxxi] you should know when to move on. It's necessary to know when something that's meant a great deal to you has reached its natural endpoint, and that the most creative choice would be to turn to what's next.

Burkeman also advises that when stumped by a life choice, you should choose "enlargement" over happiness. Major personal decisions should be made not by asking, "Will this make me happy?", but "Will this choice enlarge me or diminish me?" We're terrible at predicting what will make us happy: the question swiftly gets bogged down in our narrow preferences for security and control. But the enlargement question elicits a deeper, intuitive response. You tend to just *know* whether, say, leaving or remaining in a job, though it might bring short-term comfort, would mean cheating yourself of growth.

We don't all enjoy ideal jobs, and all jobs will have times when the going gets tough. Your job should not be a constant challenge, though, as this will too quickly grind you down. You should ask yourself if you are not enjoying your job, is this job, together with the attendant salary and status that is conferred on a DPO, still worth the investment?

The COVID 19 pandemic has challenged many data protection professionals: *What is clear is that the pandemic stripped jobs of their bells and whistles – flash offices and travel – and for some what was left was a poor work/life balance and an unfulfilling role. A lot of people realised they were in bullshit jobs that involved a lot of emails and not a lot else,* commented historian Dr Eliza Filby.[clxxxii]

A privacy professional tweeted in September 2021; *When you're a nihilist with a strong sense of justice; data protection is the hardest job in the world. It's not the mental effort that's the blocker; it's the sense of futility as you see the same mistakes being made over and over throughout the history of humanity.*[clxxxiii]

Data protection professionals aren't the only people to face daily challenges in their working lives. Dave Tomar once reflected on his job as an academic ghost-writer: *It's not a great way to earn a living. It's a burnout kind of gig. There's no end to the deadlines. It's a constant hunched-over, jaw-clenched, brow-furrowed gig. It's just not the kind of thing you can do for ever.*[clxxxiv]

What coping mechanisms should decent DPOs adopt? Popular television programme Countdown's resident lexicographer Susie Dent has testified to the effectiveness of lalochezia, or the use of swearing to alleviate stress and frustration, after discovering that her new book Word Perfect was printed with a host of typos.

There will be a time when it is appropriate to give up and move on. Moving on can mean allowing someone else's views on a particular data protection issue to prevail, or to literally move on by changing jobs, or even careers. It's your job as a DPO to offer advice. It's not your job to be accountable to the data protection supervisory authority should your organisation reject your advice and take a different course of action. So long as you have explained the risks your organisation takes by not following your recommendations, you can sleep easy. You do not "own" the data protection risks that your organisation takes. You simply need to make sure that your senior management team can blame an accountable officer should anything go wrong.

People change jobs with increasing frequency. Very early on in my working life, when I was with the Association of British Insurers, a considerable number of people I met saw their current employer as possibly their only employer during their entire working lives. They had no thoughts of ever moving on. Most of those who left their organisations did so because they were retiring, rather than moving to another organisation. The concept that career progression in the data protection sector required a change in employer (and the consequent transfer of your existing pension scheme to your new employer's pension scheme) was unheard of. Anyway, there wasn't much of a career structure for those who, in the late 1980s and early 1990s, had data protection responsibilities.

The professionalisation of the European data protection industry occurred from 2010 onwards, thanks in a large part to the US-based International Association of Privacy Professions becoming more aggressive in recruiting non-US based privacy practitioners. The IAPP initially saw itself as a conference organisation, but it soon morphed into more of a membership body. Until 2010, the concept of privacy was not something that commanded much attention from senior management teams. Data protection laws were less closely observed (and enforced by national supervisory bodies). Times have changed. In light of the behaviours of the largest tech giants, with budgets far greater than many nation states, laws were passed that required DPOs to be appointed and organisations to be liable for significant fines for non-observance. The pressure on DPOs to perform and to justify the corporate investment in the resources that are required to maintain acceptable data protection practices is high. And relentless.

Some privacy professionals are strongly motivated and have an amazing work ethic. They're very competitive and strive to excel at everything they do, whether in their personal lives or their working lives. For them, life is a glorious challenge. Work is an opportunity to push forward, to earn the respect of your fellow colleagues and to win.

Some of these people can also be extraordinarily passionate about the concept of personal privacy. They promote data protection as a fundamental human right and see no reason to give any ground or walk away from confronting anyone who challenges this concept. Decent DPOs should note that the concept of data protection as a fundamental right this is more of a European concept than it is a British concept.

European politicians decided to enforce the concept by mandating that the EU Fundamental Rights Agency, established in February 2007, promoted data protection as a fundamental right. It was reinforced in December 2007 by the signing of the Charter of Fundamental Rights of the European Union.[clxxxv] The Charter contained a new Article on the 'Protection of Personal data':

1. *Everyone has the right to the protection of personal data concerning him or her.*
2. *Such data must be processed fairly for specified purposes and on the basis of the consent of the person concerned or some other legitimate basis laid down by law. Everyone has the right of access to data which has been collected concerning him or her, and the right to have it rectified.*
3. *Compliance with these rules shall be subject to control by an independent authority.*[clxxxvi]

The British Government did not embrace this Article, nor the Charter, with much enthusiasm. The text went much further than what was considered appropriate by those who thought it was far more important to reduce the trade barriers between European countries than it was to establish a political union of EU Member

States. The opening text of the preamble was too much for many: *"The peoples of Europe, in creating an ever-closer union among them, are resolved to share a peaceful future based on common values …. To this end, it is necessary to strengthen the protection of fundamental rights in the light of changes in society, social progress and scientific and technological developments by making those rights more visible in a Charter.*[clxxxvii]

The Charter did not have full legal effect until the coming into force in December 2009 of the Treaty of Lisbon, another controversial treaty which set how much sovereignty Member States should surrender to a centralised administration. This Treaty was signed by all EU heads of state on 13 December 2007. The only head of state not to attend the televised signing ceremony was UK Prime Minister Gordon Brown. He and his delegation deliberately arrived two hours later, when all the other signatories were enjoying a celebration lunch, to sign the document alone and behind closed doors.[clxxxviii]

Decent DPOs should not take such a fundamentalist approach to protecting human rights. As far as Martin Abrams, Chief Executive and Chief Strategist of the Information Accountability Foundation, is concerned, a more balanced approach should be adopted:

While it is a fundamental right, data protection is not an absolute right. Today, proportionality most often seems to be referenced within a fundamental right (e.g. "protection of personal data") and less often as a construct that should be applied to a fuller range of fundamental rights. In short, if the GDPR requires an assessment of the full range of fundamental rights, then the proportional balance should be against this full set of rights. Picking and choosing applicable rights is inconsistent with both the GDPR and the EU Charter of Fundamental Rights. While other parts of world may not have the explicit connection as in Europe (EU Charter of Fundamental Rights and the GDPR), the implicit connection exists between privacy and other rights and by extension should be balanced in a proportional way.[clxxxix]

The more fundamentally minded DPOs tend to burn out faster than the pragmatists. They wear themselves out tilting at too many windmills. They fail to be selective to be effective. Don't fight every battle. Conserve some of your energy for the battles that really matter. These are the battles which, if you win, secure your health and happiness.

Burning bridges

Should you worry about burning bridges when you move on? While irreversible decisions tend to be more satisfying, because now there's only one direction to travel – forward into whatever choice you made – remember that the data protection community is, in relative terms, a small and notoriously indiscreet community. Someone will eventually succeed you as your organisation's DPO and your name will subsequently be associated with whatever triumphs or disasters befell your organisation as they see fit. Be careful when leaving your job and leave on good terms – you never know when you'll find yourself working with your former colleagues again. In my long career I've worked with a few individuals that are so toxic I'll make sure that I never work with them again. I won't disclose their identity in these letters. They must know who they are.

Some DPOs, of course, won't have plans to return to full time data protection work. They just plan to step down gracefully. Martin Smith, founder of the Security Awareness Special Interest Group, expressed his feelings with great eloquence as he approached the end of his career in September 2021:

I'm very nearly seventy years of age. I intend to live a healthy and fully active life until I'm at least ninety and review the situation then. That means I have twenty good summers left. Now please bear with me, dear reader, for this is not a morbid concept but quite the opposite. It's a joyous, liberating, invigorating notion. Let me explain.

As kids, our carefree school-free summers pass without thought and stretch out *into infinity. As we enter adulthood, they are hijacked by careers*, kids*, mortgages*, impecuniousness *, stress*, divorce*, redundancy*, caring for aging parents* (*delete as applicable, personally I have a full house). Without us realising, the years slip by until we count them in decades. We let them go without appreciating that they are a tightly rationed resource once spent, never to be regained.*

But as I reach my three score years and ten, I can now more accurately estimate how many I might have left. Twenty is still a good number but I must not waste a single one more of them. Hence my new perspective. From now on I'll be making the most of every year left to me to do those many things I've been putting off for too long and to explore new ideas and experiences. It's not a bucket list as such, I have no menu to work through. I've just found a new appreciation of the fragility of time. Most obviously this looks like our recent moving onto a canal boat to see the four seasons as close to nature as possible. Plans for summers to come are in the making, I might yet get to sit in Gene Krantz's chair in Mission Control, Houston...

For the reality is stark. None of us – no matter where we are on our journey through The Seven Ages of Man – have any idea just how many summers are still for us to be enjoyed. The past 18 months have shone a cold, harsh light on our individual and collective mortalities. The grand auditor is always breathing over our shoulders – realising this focuses the mind. Time is the only resource we are born with, it's the only thing we have to use and barter with to survive on this earth, and when it runs out our time is (literally) up.

I wish I'd been wish I'd been more aware of this a long time ago, but that ship has long passed. For now, I'll just concentrate on the future and make sure Jo and I squeeze every drop out of our next twenty summers. And autumns, winters and springs. No matter where you are on the continuum of life, I commend this approach to you. ^{cxc}

Now my time is up, too. I'm ready to move on and I'm ready to pass my data protection baton to you.

With my warmest regards,

Martin

ABOUT THE AUTHOR

Martin Hoskins has been a data protection professional for over 30 years, providing a strategic and practical approach on privacy, banking, child safety, insurance, interception, law enforcement and marketing issues. Having held senior operational privacy roles with some of Britain's largest and well-known companies, he has worked extensively in organisations that were undertaking significant internal changes and privacy programmes.

In 2012 Martin was appointed Specialist Advisor to the Joint Committee on the Draft Communications Data Bill and returned to Parliament in 2016 as Specialist Advisor to the Joint Committee on the Draft Investigatory Powers Bill. He has also given evidence before various Parliamentary Select Committees. Having served on industry working panels administered by the CBI, mobile telecommunications industry, Home Office, Ministry of Justice, Association of Chief Police Officers and the financial services trade bodies, he maintains close links with fellow professions across a wide range of fields.

Martin has a degree in Government, Politics and Modern History. He is also a Licentiate of the Chartered Insurance Institute and is a holder of the BCS/ISEB data protection practitioner certificate. Martin is also a Freeman of the City of London.

REFERENCES

Introduction

[i] https://iapp.org/resources/article/gdpr-at-two-expert-perspectives/?mkt_tok=eyJpljoiTVdNM05HTXhPVFkzWkdObSIsInQiOiJcL2ZQZE1SV2c1anI0YTlGU2RadXRwZmV2ME5CTWU0cWhqSmZQN0pYcnNoSTZUZZmQnhtaDFTXC9DV3JGc1ltXC9CZWY3S1ViNXErVmtuTlwvWlVhY1VwRm55N0ZHZ3NJbmdTWG9DU1lmbDFlBb1JQWU5rZ8nBHNzhjTkFpd0w1RWM0UE0ifQ%3D%3D

[ii] https://www.axel-voss-europa.de/wp-content/uploads/2021/05/GDPR-2.0-ENG.pdf

[iii] GDPR Recital 26

[iv] https:/news/a/a-guide-to-the-us-anonymization-standards/?mkt_tok=MTM4LUVaTSOw...https://iapp.org/news/a/a-guide-to-the-eus-unclear-anonymization-standards/?mkt_tok=MTM4LUVaTS0wNDIAAAF-ShiUuet61LGssj6q8tuEPPLgmC79hdKa5jgD6e8_zkeLiSpe-ZtKBVcNdXQifSz5feEDmS2Ai_GlnVPP8Okadb-nthjrEAYMdI5Sfa9RWbiq

[v] https://ico.org.uk/about-the-ico/ico-and-stakeholder-consultations/ico-call-for-views-anonymisation-pseudonymisation-and-privacy-enhancing-technologies-guidance/

[vi] Opinion 4/2007 on the concept of personal data https://ec.europa.eu/justice/article-29/documentation/opinion-recommendation/files/2007/wp136_en.pdf

[vii] Opinion 5/2014 0n anonymisation techniques https://ec.europa.eu/justice/article-29/documentation/opinion-recommendation/files/2014/wp216_en.pdf

[viii] IAPP article: A guide to the EU's unclear anonymisation standards by Andrew Burt, Alfred Rossi & Sophie Stalla-Bourdillon https://iapp.org/news/a/a-guide-to-the-eus-unclear-anonymization-standards/?mkt_tok=MTM4LUVaTS0wNDIAAAF-ShiUuet61LGssj6q8tuEPPLgmC79hdKa5jgD6e8_zkeLiSpe-ZtKBVcNdXQifSz5feEDmS2Ai_GlnVPP8Okadb-nthjrEAYMdI5Sfa9RWbiq

Letter 1: Doing the right thing

[ix] Tim Turner, Data Protection Officer Guide 2017
https://2040training.co.uk/wp-content/uploads/2017/12/DPO-Guide.pdf
[x] Privacy tech's third generation: A review of the emerging privacy tech sector   https://fpf.org/wp-content/uploads/2021/06/FPF-PTA-Report_Digital.pdf

[xi] Sir Henry (John) Newbolt (1862-1938) Poems: New and Old (Dodo Press), 2008

[xii] Harry Ognall, A Life of Crime, the memoirs of a High Court Judge, William Collins, 2017 ISBN 978-0-00-826748-3 ch7 p 143
[xiii] https://www.theguardian.com/lifeandstyle/2020/sep/04/oliver-burkemans-last-column-the-eight-secrets-to-a-fairly-fulfilled-life

Letter 2: Applying the key data protection principles
[xiv] GDPR Article 37(5)
[xv] GDPR Articles 6 & 9
[xvi] GDPR Recital 39
[xvii] GDPR Articles 13 & 14

Letter 3: Translating the law into practical steps
[xviii] GDPR Article 12 & Recital 58
[xix] https://ico.org.uk/about-the-ico/news-and-events/news-and-blogs/2020/10/ico-takes-enforcement-action-against-experian-after-data-broking-investigation/
[xx] iapp.org/news/a/irish-dpc-whatsapp-d
[xxi] GDPR Article 5(d)
[xxii] GDPR Articles 5.1(f) & 32
[xxiii] GDPR Recital 1
[xxiv] GDPR Article 5(1)(f)
[xxv] GDPR Article 5.2
[xxvi]

https://www.huntonak.com/files/webupload/CIPL_Galway_Accountability_Paper.pdf
[xxvii] https://globalprivacyassembly.org/wp-content/uploads/2015/02/The-Madrid-Resolution.pdf
[xxviii] GDPR Article 25

xxix https://ico.org.uk/action-weve-taken/enforcement/british-airways/
xxx https://ico.org.uk/action-weve-taken/enforcement/marriott-international-inc/
xxxi Data Protection Act 2018
xxxii GDPR Article 28.1
xxxiii GDPR Recital 63
xxxiv Twitter user @TessaRDavis on 14/9/21
xxxvhttps://assets.publishing.service.gov.uk/government/uploads/system/uploads/attachment_data/file/1016395/Data_Reform_Consultation_Document__Accessible_.pdf para 186
xxxvi Freedom of Information and Data Protection (Appropriate Limit and Fees) Regulations 2004
xxxvii GDPR Article 21.2-3
xxxviii GDPR Article 21-22
xxxix GDPR Article 89.1
xl https://ico.org.uk/for-organisations/childrens-code-hub/
xli https://www.wired.co.uk/article/age-appropriate-design-code-big-tech
xlii GDPR Recital 68
xliii More guidance is available in the Open Data Handbook, published by Open Knowledge international
xlivhttps://www.linkedin.com/feed/hashtag/?keywords=gdpr&highlightedUpdateUrns=urn%3Ali%3Aactivity%3A6828975622434406400
xlvhttps://www.linkedin.com/feed/hashtag/?keywords=gdpr&highlightedUpdateUrns=urn%3Ali%3Aactivity%3A6828975622434406400

Letter 4: Accepting risks
xlvi https://www.theguardian.com/lifeandstyle/2020/sep/04/oliver-burkemans-last-column-the-eight-secrets-to-a-fairly-fulfilled-life

xlvii https://ico.org.uk/media/about-the-ico/documents/2618304/office-risk-assessment-covid-19-170820-london.pdf
xlviii https://ico.org.uk/for-organisations/guide-to-data-protection/guide-to-the-general-data-protection-regulation-gdpr/accountability-and-governance/data-protection-impact-assessments/
xlix https://ec.europa.eu/newsroom/article29/items/611236
l https://ico.org.uk/media/for-organisations/documents/2620329/explaining-decisions-made-with-ai-summary.pdf

li https://spectrum.ieee.org/stop-calling-everything-ai-machinelearning-pioneer-says

lii @1Br0wn tweet 7 September 2021

liii https://inplp.com/latest-news/article/the-estonian-data-protection-authority-issued-guidance-on-the-definition-of-large-scale-processing/

liv https://ico.org.uk/for-organisations/childrens-code-hub/

lv https://teachprivacy.com/privacy-harms/

lvi https://ico.org.uk/for-organisations/guide-to-data-protection/guide-to-the-general-data-protection-regulation-gdpr/accountability-and-governance/data-protection-impact-assessments/

lvii https://ec.europa.eu/newsroom/article29/items/611236

lviii https://ico.org.uk/for-organisations/accountability-framework/

Letter 5: Priorities

lix GDPR Article 5.2

lx GDPR Recital 74

lxi https://ico.org.uk/media/about-the-ico/policies-and-procedures/4018498/data-protection-policy-2109.pdf

lxii

https://www.informationpolicycentre.com/uploads/5/7/1/0/5710428
1/slides_-_cipl-ico_accountability_toolkit_roundtable_-
_11_feb_2020.pdf

lxiii https://ico.org.uk/for-organisations/accountability-framework/

lxiv

https://www.informationpolicycentre.com/uploads/5/7/1/0/5710428
1/slides_-_cipl-ico_accountability_toolkit_roundtable_-
_11_feb_2020.pdf

Letter 6: Regulators

lxv GDPR Article 63

lxvi https://news.bloomberglaw.com/tech-and-telecom-law/eus-broken-gdpr-needs-fixing-departing-privacy-chief-warns

lxvii Data Protection Code of Practice, Association of British Insurers, Dec 1993

lxviii Guidance Book for the Financial Services Industries on the Data Protection Act 1998, published by various financial services trade bodies, Aug 2000

lxix
https://www.engage.hoganlovells.com/knowledgeservices/news/five-conclusions-from-the-uk-icos-british-airways-fine

lxx https://techcrunch.com/2020/10/16/uks-ico-downgrades-british-airways-data-breach-fine-to-20m-after-originally-setting-it-at-184m/

lxxi https://ico.org.uk/media/action-weve-taken/mpns/2620171/mermaids-mpn-20210705.pdf

lxxii Data Protection Act 2018

lxxiii https://www.wsj.com/articles/outgoing-u-k-privacy-regulator-wants-global-consensus-on-data-disputes-11631698201?mod=searchresults_pos1&page=1&mkt_tok=MTM4LUV
aTS0wNDIAAAF_iXAV1g-
3VE05TorTuRWqlbDE50qmIKbhWeoqJeNWUl6g2vBburzNoGrU4OcXB
WHg0VCi6sJKCHkyicsEwFQw8AETfazms1ytMBAp-0q6QLHd

lxxivhttps://assets.publishing.service.gov.uk/government/uploads/syste
m/uploads/attachment_data/file/1016395/Data_Reform_Consultatio
n_Document__Accessible_.pdf

lxxv *https://dpnetwork.org.uk/uk-data-regime-change-consultation-12-highlights/?utm_source=Data+Protection+Network&utm_campaign=0
d997185b6-
EMAIL_CAMPAIGN_2021_09_13_09_12&utm_medium=email&utm_te
rm=0_294c5d36b6-0d997185b6-227713689*

lxxvi https://iapp.org/news/a/changing-direction-uk-consults-reforms-to-its-data-protection-law/?mkt_tok=MTM4LUVaTS0wNDIAAAGAI-
Y4a548Zyh17_-dLtrD4b79Cx3PyekqNkTRTjn6JTbzt09HlxjwpIExU18b-
dfX37uuaRwPehcOXPN2PcoFfnqQsmBGvkhi3XGdkhHj4GAA

lxxvii https://amberhawk.typepad.com/amberhawk/2021/11/ministers-want-to-pull-the-strings-and-rein-in-the-icos-independence.html

lxxviii https://iapp.org/news/a/changing-direction-uk-consults-reforms-to-its-data-protection-law/?mkt_tok=MTM4LUVaTS0wNDIAAAGAI-
Y4a548Zyh17_-dLtrD4b79Cx3PyekqNkTRTjn6JTbzt09HlxjwpIExU18b-
dfX37uuaRwPehcOXPN2PcoFfnqQsmBGvkhi3XGdkhHj4GAA

lxxix https://amberhawk.typepad.com/amberhawk/2021/11/ministers-want-to-pull-the-strings-and-rein-in-the-icos-independence.html

lxxx ibid

lxxxi ibid

lxxxii ibid

[lxxxiii] https://iapp.org/news/a/changing-direction-uk-consults-reforms-to-its-data-protection-law/?mkt_tok=MTM4LUVaTS0wNDIAAAGAI-Y4a548Zyh17_-dLtrD4b79Cx3PyekqNkTRTjn6JTbzt09HlxjwpIExU18b-dfX37uuaRwPehcOXPN2PcoFfnqQsmBGvkhi3XGdkhHj4GAA

[lxxxiv] ibid

[lxxxv] ibid

[lxxxvi] Ibid

[lxxxvii] ibid

[lxxxviii] ibid

[lxxxix]

https://amberhawk.typepad.com/amberhawk/2021/11/ministers-want-to-pull-the-strings-and-rein-in-the-icos-independence.html

Letter 7: Overwhelming workloads

[xc] https://www.dpocentre.com/evolving-role-of-the-dpo-2-years-on/

[xci] Twitter user @SandreJ

[xcii] Twitter user @neil_neilzone

[xciii] My Booky Wook, Russell Brand Hodder & Stoughton 2007 ISBN 978 0 340 93615 3 p21

[xciv] https://www.theguardian.com/books/2021/sep/01/four-thousand-weeks-by-oliver-burkeman-review-a-brief-treatise-on-time

[xcv] Four Thousand Weeks: Time and How to Use, published by Bodley Head, 2021

[xcvi] https://www.telegraph.co.uk/health-fitness/mind/six-ways-modern-life-making-us-unhappy-can-cope/

[xcvii] Compliance Budget: Managing Security Behaviour in Organisations, a paper by Adam Beautement, M. Angela Sasse of UCL & Mike Wonham of Hewlett Packard
https://discovery.ucl.ac.uk/id/eprint/1301853/1/compliance_budgetfinal.pdf

Letter 8: Teamwork

[xcviii] GDPR Article 39

[xcix] GDPR Article 32.1

[c] GDPR Article 38.6

[ci] https://www.lda.bayern.de/media/pm2016_08.pdf

[cii] https://www.fieldfisher.com/en/services/privacy-security-and-information/privacy-security-and-information-law-blog/heads-of-compliance-legal-step-down-as-dpo

[ciii] GDPR Article 39.2

[civ] GDPR Articles 37 - 39
[cv] https://boostandco.com/seven-leadership-style-covid-19/?utm_campaign=CBILS&utm_medium=Social_Media&utm_source=linkedin_paid&utm_term=cbils

Letter 9: Education & continuing professional development
[cvi] GDPR Article 37.5
[cvii] https://www.dataprotection.ie/en/organisations/know-your-obligations/data-protection-officrs/guidance-appropriate-qualifications
[cviii] https://www.linkedin.com/in/datasuperhero/ 6 August 2021

[cix] ibid
[cx] Tim Turner, Data Protection Officer Guide 2017
https://2040training.co.uk/wp-content/uploads/2017/12/DPO-Guide.pdf
[cxi] https//privacyassociation.org/certify/cipp
[cxii] https://www.northumbria.ac.uk/study-at-northumbria/courses/information-rights-law-and-practice-dtpilp6/#modules
[cxiii] Email to the author, January 2016
[cxiv] https://www.dlapiperdataprotection.com/?t=law&c=RU
[cxv] https://academic.oup.com/idpl/article-abstract/7/1/70/3782688?redirectedFrom=fulltext
[cxvi] https://www.cpdpconferences.org
[cxvii] https://www.privacylaws.com
[cxviii] https://iapp.org/news/daily-dashboard/
[cxix] GDPR Article 37

Letter 10: Career development
[cxx] Section 7 of the Data Protection Act 2018 defines what a 'public authority' and a 'public body' are for the purposes of the GDPR

[cxxi] https://ec.europa.eu/newsroom/article29/items/612048
[cxxii] https://inplp.com/latest-news/article/the-estonian-data-protection-authority-issued-guidance-on-the-definition-of-large-scale-processing/
[cxxiii] https://www.gov.uk/government/consultations/data-a-new-direction
[cxxiv] https://ico.org.uk/media/about-the-ico/consultation-responses/4018588/dcms-consultation-response-20211006.pdf

cxxv GDPR Article 39

cxxvi GDPR Article 38.6

cxxvii https://www.lda.bayern.de/media/pm2016_08.pdf

cxxviii https://www.fieldfisher.com/en/services/privacy-security-and-information/privacy-security-and-information-law-blog/heads-of-compliance-legal-step-down-as-dpo

cxxix Blue Sky Thinking, is it time to stop work taking over or lives, by Elle Hunt, The Guardian 4 Oct 2020. https://www.theguardian.com/money/2020/oct/04/blue-sky-thinking-is-it-time-to-stop-work-taking-over-our-lives

cxxx https://www.linkedin.com/news/story/i-had-no-idea-how-to-get-promoted-4431313/

cxxxi Ibid

cxxxii https://www.linkedin.com/in/fraser-merrifield-7b54524/

cxxxiii Data Protection Act 2018 Schedule 2

Letter 11: Toxic relationships

cxxxiv https://ico.org.uk/for-organisations/guide-to-data-protection/guide-to-the-general-data-protection-regulation-gdpr/right-of-access/when-can-we-refuse-to-comply-with-a-request/

cxxxv https://www.careercontessa.com/advice/office-bullies/

cxxxvi https://www.acas.org.uk/disciplinary-and-grievance-procedures

cxxxvii https://ico.org.uk/media/about-the-ico/policies-and-procedures/1853/data-protection-regulatory-action-policy.pdf#:~:text=In%20line%20with%20our%20information%20rights%20strategy%2C%20the,only%20at%20cases%20in%20which%20action%20is%20needed.

cxxxviii https://edpb.europa.eu/news/news_en

cxxxix Warren v DSG Retail Ltd [2021] EWHC 2168 (QB) Para 22

cxl Ibid, para 27

cxli https://panopticonblog.com/2021/07/30/important-new-high-court-judgment-on-data-breach-litigation/#more-4073

cxlii Lloyd v Google LLC [2021] UKSC 50

cxliii https://iapp.org/news/a/uk-supreme-court-halts-billion-dollar-privacy-class-action-against-google/?mkt_tok=MTM4LUVaTS0wNDIAAAGAqjYzcCqKS0VXw8hme-kEJtMZ3EIIM5CFTmhJvtUXYEkewWWmksbYDqbSepoC6v8usAXwAaERo0olVS0grRDU-r_VqrsJRauRAXnBQqadYf3ID0

cxliv https://www.bbc.co.uk/news/technology-59221037

_____

Letter 12: International issues

cxlv https://www.dlapiperdataprotection.com/?t=law&c=RU

cxlvi   https://www.cipil.law.cam.ac.uk/projects/european-data-protection-laws-freedom-expression

cxlviihttps://assets.publishing.service.gov.uk/government/uploads/system/uploads/attachment_data/file/1016395/Data_Reform_Consultation_Document__Accessible_.pdf

cxlviii Asia's privacy reform Bills: various speeds, Graham Greenleaf (2021) 171 Privacy Laws & Business International Report 26-29 https://papers.ssrn.com/sol3/papers.cfm?abstract_id=3899557

cxlix https://ec.europa.eu/info/law/law-topic/data-protection/international-dimension-data-protection/standard-contractual-clauses-scc/standard-contractual-clauses-international-transfers_en

cl https://edpb.europa.eu/news/news/2021/edpb-adopts-final-version-recommendations-supplementary-measures-letter-eu_en

cli https://www.essentialguarantees.com/scc/

clii https://www.huntonprivacyblog.com/2020/09/02/german-dpa-issues-guidance-on-data-transfers-following-schrems-ii/

cliii https://www.privacylaws.com/int172germany

cliv https://ico.org.uk/about-the-ico/ico-and-stakeholder-consultations/ico-consultation-on-data-transferred-outside-of-the-uk/

clv ibid

clvi https://fpf.org/blog/upcoming-data-protection-rulings-in-the-eu-an-overview-of-cjeu-pending-cases/

clvii ibid

clviii https://curia.europa.eu/jcms/upload/docs/application/pdf/2021-04/ra_pan_2020_en.pdf

Letter 13: Open-mindedness

clix https://www.theguardian.com/lifeandstyle/2020/sep/04/oliver-burkemans-last-column-the-eight-secrets-to-a-fairly-fulfilled-life

clx https://www.ourcivilisation.com/decline/badlaws.htm

clxi https://www.theguardian.com/books/2018/sep/02/why-we-get-the-wrong-politicians-isabel-hardman-review Review of 'Why We Get the Wrong Politicians' by Isobel Hardman, Atlantic Books

clxii http://www.legislation.gov.uk/ukpga/1991/65/contents

clxiii https://www.bva.co.uk/news-and-blog/blog-article/did-dangerous-dogs-really-just-disappear-overnight-the-dangerous-dogs-act-30-years-on/

clxiv https://www.thesun.co.uk/news/1577023/hundreds-of-danger-dogs-put-down-needlessly-because-of-the-way-they-look-claims-rspca/

clxv Directive 2002/58/EC of the European Parliament and of the Council of 12 July 2002 concerning the processing of personal data and the protection of privacy in the electronic communications sector (Directive on privacy and electronic communications).

clxvi ibid Article 5.3.

clxvii Directive 2009/136/EC

clxviii

https://edps.europa.eu/sites/edp/files/publication/dir_2009_136_en.pdf Article 5.3

clxix The UK introduced the amendments on 25 May 2011 through The Privacy and Electronic Communications (EC Directive) (Amendment) Regulations 2011.

clxx

https://edps.europa.eu/sites/edp/files/publication/dir_2009_136_en.pdf

clxxi https://www.verisign.com/en_GB/domain-names/online/implement/what-are-cookies/index.xhtml

clxxii Ibid

clxxiii Ibid

clxxiv https://assets.publishing.service.gov.uk/government/uploads/system/uploads/attachment_data/file/1016395/Data_Reform_Consultation_Document__Accessible_.pdf

clxxv https://www.brainyquote.com/quotes/edmund_burke_149703

clxxvi https://amberhawk.typepad.com

clxxvii https://panopticonblog.com/2021/08/31/new-cjeu-judgment-on-intermediary-liability/#more-4082

clxxviii The Data Privacy Law of Brexit: Theories of Preference Change by Paul M Schwartz [Jefferson E. Peyser Professor of Law, UC Berkeley School of Law; Director, Berkeley Center for Law & Technology] Published in the journal Theoretical Inquiries in Law, Vol 22.2:111:2021

clxxix https://committees.parliament.uk/committee/378/digital-culture-media-and-sport-committee/news/157290/mps-question-governments-preferred-candidate-for-information-commissioner/
clxxx http://www.kiplingsociety.co.uk/poems_runnymede.htm

Letter 14: Never give up?
clxxxi https://www.theguardian.com/lifeandstyle/2020/sep/04/oliver-burkemans-last-column-the-eight-secrets-to-a-fairly-fulfilled-life

clxxxii https://www.telegraph.co.uk/news/0/generation-resignation-millennials-refusing-return-office/
clxxxiii @MissIG_Geek tweet 1 September 2021
clxxxiv https://www.turnitin.com/blog/straight-talk-from-an-essay-mill-insider-part-1

clxxxv https://fra.europa.eu/sites/default/files/charter-of-fundamental-rights-of-the-european-union-2007-c_303-01_en.pdf
clxxxvi Charter of Fundamental Rights of the European Union Article 8
clxxxvii https://fra.europa.eu/sites/default/files/charter-of-fundamental-rights-of-the-european-union-2007-c_303-01_en.pdf
clxxxviii https://www.theguardian.com/uk/2007/dec/13/politics.world
clxxxix https://informationaccountability.org/2020/08/data-protection-should-be-proportional-to-other-individual-rights/
cxc https://www.thesasig.com/blog/blog_24/

Printed in Great Britain
by Amazon

72504371R00159